Grand Diplôme Cooking Course

Volume 3

Grand Diplôme Cooking Course

A Danbury Press Book

The Danbury Press

a division of Grolier Enterprises, Inc.

Robert B. Clarke   Publisher

This book has been adapted from the Grand Diplôme Cooking Course, originally published by Purnell Cookery, U.S.A.

Purnell Grand Diplôme Editorial Board

Rosemary Hume and Muriel Downes
Principals, London Cordon Bleu Cookery
School, England

Anne Willan	Editor
Eleanor Noderer	Associate Editor
Sheryl Julian	Assistant Editor
John Paton	Managing Editor
José Northey	Co-ordinating Editor
Peter Leather	Art Editor
Charles F. Turgeon	Wine Consultant

Library of Congress Catalog Card Number: 72-13896
© B.P.C. Publishing, 1971, and
© Phoebus Publishing, 1972.
Filmsetting by Petty and Sons Ltd., Leeds, England.
Printed in the United States of America

234567899876543

All recipes have been tested either at the Cordon Bleu Cookery School in London or in our U.S. test kitchens.

Note: all recipe quantities in this book serve 4 people unless otherwise stated.

Contents

All recipes have been tested either at the Cordon Bleu Cookery School in London or in our U.S. test kitchens.

Note: all recipe quantities in this book serve 4 people unless otherwise stated.

From the Editor

Find which herb gives flavor to Béarnaise sauce, learn the difference between a ragoût and a blanquette and read about the exotic origins of saffron, the most valuable spice in the world. These are just three of the topics covered in the third Volume of your Grand Diplôme Cooking Course, created by the Cordon Bleu Cookery School in London from the methods and recipes taught to their students for over 30 years.

Take your pick of **Shellfish** favorites like stuffed clams, scallops parisienne and scampi à la crème or be tempted by some superbly rich **Velouté, Bisque and Iced Soups** that include almond and grape soup and chilled shrimp bisque. Compete with the best of the barbecue buffs with the help of detailed advice on **Broiling Meat and Fish** with ideas for sauces and simple accompaniments. When it's time to move indoors, **Stews** come into their own — delicate fricassée of rabbit, pungent goulash glowing with paprika, and down-to-earth Irish stew.

Make the most of the **Fresh Fruits** in season with strawberries Romanoff, blueberry soup or tartelettes coeur à la crème — even their names are mouth-watering. Fruits are also featured in a lesson on **Flans** — colorful open-faced pies — together with their savory cousins filled with fish, eggs and a variety of vegetables. **Herbs and Spices** are indispensable to good cooking; they add interest to simple dishes and subtlety to sophisticated ones, so glance at their history before turning to charts that show their best uses.

The four Grand Diplôme **Menus** that appear in this, as in every Volume, include a barbecue party, a buffet for 12, a quick gourmet dinner and a special supper that includes curried chicken and crème caramel. At the back of the book you'll find some hints on **Large-scale Cooking** and a guide to the basics of how to **Measure Ingredients** and select the right **Oven Temperature**.

The remaining Volumes 4–20 of Grand Diplôme cover every aspect of cooking. You'll find features on foreign food from countries as far apart as Italy and Indonesia, menus for occasions varying from an intimate dinner to a wedding buffet and lessons on everything from carving meat to whipping up that triumph of French cuisine, the soufflé.

Please join us and enjoy cooking the Grand Diplôme way. Bon Appétit!

Anne Willan

Steaks Morateur are pan-fried and covered with a piquant sauce; serve with French fries and green beans (recipe is on page 12)

A Special Meal
that's quick to make

This menu is designed to cut corners but not quality. Mushroom soup, fillet steak with anchovy sauce and cherry pudding are quick to make, with few ingredients, yet their originality makes them right for a special occasion.

The Côte de Beaune Villages wine suggested for the steak is, as its name indicates, a blend of harvest red wines from vineyards in various townships surrounding Beaune, the 'capital of Burgundy'. An equally pleasing light red from California is the Pinot St. George which is raised chiefly in the Napa Valley.

Mushroom Soup

Steaks Morateur
French Fried Potatoes
Green Beans   Green Salad

Cherry Pudding

∽

Red wine – Côte de Beaune Villages (Burgundy)
or
Pinot St. George (California)

TIMETABLE

Morning
Pit and cook fresh cherries; drain canned cherries. Make and bake cherry pudding but do not add meringue.

Wash green beans and, if small, halve them; trim and French them (cut in fine diagonal slices). Store in a plastic bag in refrigerator.

Prepare potatoes for French-frying and soak whole in cold water. Do not refrigerate.

Wash salad greens, store in plastic bag or container in refrigerator.

Make salad dressing.

Prepare mushroom soup and refrigerate.

Make anchovy butter.

Assemble equipment for final cooking from 6:30 p.m. for dinner around 8 p.m.

Order of Work

6:30
Set oven at 300°F for cherry pudding. Make meringue.
Bake at once if pudding is to be served cold.

7:00
Put soup in pan ready to reheat. Cut potatoes. Put plates and dishes to warm.

7:30
Bake cherry pudding if to be served hot.
Cook green beans.
Give the French fries their first frying and drain.

7:45
Toss salad with dressing.
Fry steaks and make the sauce. Keep warm. Pour sauce over just before serving.
Reheat the soup.

8:00
Serve soup.
Fry French fries 1–2 minutes to brown just before serving.

You will find that **cooking times** given in the individual recipes for these dishes have sometimes been adapted in the timetable to help you when cooking and serving this menu as a party meal.

Appetizer

Mushroom Soup

2 cups (½ lb) mushrooms
3 tablespoons butter
2 medium onions, chopped
2 tablespoons flour
5 cups chicken stock
salt and pepper
1 tablespoon rice
1 bay leaf
2 tablespoons chopped watercress (for garnish)

Method
Wipe mushrooms with a damp cloth and trim stems level with the caps. Finely chop the stems and thinly slice the caps.

Melt 2 tablespoons of the butter in a pan, add onions, mushroom slices and chopped stems. Cover with a piece of buttered foil, buttered side pressed down onto the vegetables, and the lid, and cook over a low heat for 5 minutes. Remove pan from heat, take off lid and foil and add remaining butter. When melted, blend in flour evenly and add stock. Season with salt and pepper and cook, stirring constantly, until mixture boils. Add rice and bay leaf, cover and simmer 15–20 minutes.

Before serving, remove bay leaf, season to taste and sprinkle chopped watercress on top.

Choosing Mushrooms
It has been possible to buy **mushrooms** in most parts of this country only within the last 25–30 years. Today they are grown on mushroom farms all year round. Mushrooms range in size from 1 inch across cap to 4–5 inches in diameter, but freshness, not size, is the best indication of good flavor. Choose firm mushrooms, light in color with the ridges underneath the cap still hugging the stem. Keep these caps in good shape by cutting the stem flush with the base of the cap; slice vertically, right through cap and top of stem. (Do not discard stems; use in soups, stuffings, or stews.) 1 lb mushrooms will serve four people as a vegetable; ½ lb is plenty for most garnishes or for seasoning.

Delicious fresh mushroom soup, garnished with watercress, is served in individual bowls

Entrée

Steaks Morateur

4 fillet steaks, about 1 inch
thick
1 tablespoon butter
1 shallot, finely chopped
½ cup dry white wine
3 tablespoons anchovy butter

Plenty of French fried potatoes
go best with this dish. For the
hot vegetable, serve green
beans and/or a tossed green
salad on salad plates.

Method
Heat a frying pan or skillet
for 2–3 minutes before cooking begins. (A heavy cast-
iron frying pan gives best
results; if an aluminum one
is used, put 1 teaspoon salad
oil in it before heating.)

Add butter and, when
foaming, put in steaks. Press
them down well with a
spatula and lower heat slightly. Cook steaks for about 3
minutes or until well browned,
turn to the other side and
cook 3 minutes longer (for
rare meat). Remove from heat
and put steaks on a warm
platter.

Stir chopped shallot into
pan, lower heat, and cook 2–3
minutes. Pour in wine and
cook until it is reduced by half.
Stir in anchovy butter and simmer 2–3 minutes longer.
Pour sauce over steaks and
serve. If serving an appetizer first, cook the steaks for a
slightly shorter time and keep
them warm; pour sauce over
just before serving them (see
timetable, page 10).

Anchovy Butter

Soften 2 tablespoons un-
salted butter on a plate
with a small spatula.
In a mortar and pestle
crush or pound 2–3
anchovy fillets (previously
soaked in milk to remove
excess saltiness), and add
these to the butter along
with freshly ground pep-
per. Blend in 1 teaspoon
anchovy paste to accent
the flavor and give a delicate pink color.

Fry the steaks over high heat
until well browned (about 3
minutes each side)

Pound the soaked anchovy
fillets in a mortar and pestle
for anchovy butter

Dessert

Cherry Pudding

1 lb fresh red cherries, pitted or
1 can (16 oz) pitted red
cherries
2½ tablespoons sugar
1¼ cups milk
1 cup fresh white breadcrumbs
2 egg yolks
grated rind of ½ lemon
1 cup heavy cream (to serve)
– optional

For meringue topping
2 egg whites
¼ cup sugar

Soufflé dish (1 quart capacity)

If possible fresh red cherries
should be used for this dessert; if using canned ones,
reduce the sugar in the pudding to 1 tablespoon.

Method
Put fresh cherries in a pan,
add a little of the sugar, cover
and cook over a low heat for
2–3 minutes; drain canned
cherries.

Scald milk, pour it over
breadcrumbs and let mixture
stand for 5 minutes. Stir in
egg yolks, remaining sugar
and grated lemon rind. Drain
cherries, add them to the mixture and spoon into soufflé
dish. Stand dish in a water
bath and bake in a moderate
oven (350°F) for 30–40
minutes or until the mixture is
just set. Remove pudding
from oven and reduce tem-
perature to low (300°F).

To prepare meringue top-
ping: beat egg whites until
they hold a soft shape. Beat
in 1 teaspoon of the sugar
and, when whites are quite
firm, quickly fold in the remaining sugar. Pile meringue

on top of pudding, sprinkle a
little extra sugar on top and
let stand for 4–5 minutes at
room temperature. Bake
pudding in heated oven for
30 minutes. Serve hot or cold,
with heavy cream, if you like.

Add the drained cherries to
the milk, egg and breadcrumb
mixture before baking

Carefully pile the meringue on
top of baked cherry mixture
before returning pudding to a
low oven to bake until crisp

Cherry pudding, with a meringue topping, may be served hot or cold

Paprika goulash is an Hungarian stew, generally made with beef, and flavored with paprika and peppers (recipe is on page 19)

HOW TO STEW

Stews have somehow acquired a reputation of being inelegant and unappetizing. But sophisticated stews like blanquette of veal or navarin of lamb are gourmet dishes, and even the most fastidious cooks must admit that a hearty dish like Irish stew makes a splendid family meal.

Stewing means to cook food gently in liquid; it is usually associated with meat, although fish, vegetables and fruit can also be stewed.

In general, inexpensive cuts of meat require long, slow cooking, which helps to tenderize and bring out flavor. Cuts with a slight marbling of fat are excellent stewed because the marbling makes the meat more succulent.

A stew can be white or brown. In a white stew, sometimes called a fricassée, the meat is not browned but blanched to whiten it and remove strong flavors before cooking. The liquid is often thickened after the meat is cooked or towards the end of cooking as in Irish stew — when the softened potatoes thicken the gravy. A white stew is usually cooked on top of the stove.

In a brown stew, sometimes called a ragoût, meat is browned with or without vegetables and a little flour is stirred in just before the stock is added. It may be cooked on top of the stove or in the oven.

In both brown and white stews the liquid must never get hotter than simmering point as boiling will toughen the meat.

PREPARATION OF STEWS

White stew. Cover meat with cold water in a pan, add salt and — for veal or rabbit — a slice of lemon to whiten the meat. Blanch by bringing slowly to a boil, skimming, draining and refreshing in cold water to wash away the scum. Return to the pan and add the liquid specified in the recipe (usually just enough to cover the meat).

Veal or chicken stock, not water, should be used if possible, because stock makes a much better sauce. Keep the pan covered throughout the cooking.

Brown stew. The pan is very important in making a brown stew. Choose a Dutch oven, a thick, enameled iron pan or a flameproof casserole so the stew can be cooked and served in the same container. Alternatively, brown the meat in a skillet or frying pan and transfer it to a casserole, but make the sauce or gravy in the skillet to avoid losing any juices.

Cut the meat (without bone) into 2 inch cubes, leaving a little fat. Gristle appears only in beef shank or chuck so ignore any white streaks as this is fat, not gristle. Cuts with bone should be divided into slightly larger pieces.

Heat the pan or casserole well before adding drippings or oil. Put in just enough meat to cover the bottom of the pan and leave room to turn the pieces comfortably. Fry on full heat for beef (not so high for lamb or veal) until the meat is evenly browned (about 2–3 minutes). Turn each piece and brown on the other side. Do not fry for longer than 7 minutes.

Take out the meat and keep hot. Add vegetables called for in the recipe, lower heat and cook until lightly browned. Pour off excess fat, leaving 2 tablespoons. Add flour (about 1 tablespoon for 3 cups stock), using slightly less if stock is jellied. Cook flour 2–3 minutes until colored, scraping it gently from bottom of pan or casserole with a metal spoon.

Add stock (1½ cups for 1 lb solid meat). It is better to add two-thirds of the given quantity first, and bring just to a boil. Replace meat, then add remaining stock so it comes just below level of meat. Add specified seasonings, herbs etc., cover pan or casserole tightly and cook as stated in the recipe.

If cooking a stew ahead of time, transfer it to another container so it cools quickly; when reheating, bring just to a boil and then keep warm (boiling kills any bacteria which may be present).

In a stew a scant ½ lb solid meat like steak should serve one person, but allow more if the cut includes bone, as with neck or breast.

The following cuts are good for stewing:

Beef: chuck, round, flank, and arm steak; short ribs; plate, hind shank.

Lamb: neck, breast; shank; riblets.

Veal: breast; shoulder; shank; neck.

TYPES OF STEW

Fricassée describes various stews of meat, poultry, fish or vegetables, usually made with a white stock. In France this term refers almost exclusively to a poultry dish in a white sauce.

Ragoût (brown) contains pieces of meat, poultry or fish lightly browned and then slowly cooked in stock with vegetables.

Salmis is a type of ragoût, usually of game or poultry. The meat is first lightly roasted, then cut up and gently simmered for a short time in a rich brown sauce.

Blanquette of lamb, veal, chicken or rabbit is made as a white ragoût, enriched with egg yolks and cream and sometimes garnished with small onions and mushrooms.

Navarin is the French word for a mutton or lamb stew made with root vegetables. Certain vegetables are good stewed alone, especially white ones such as onions, celery, root or Jerusalem artichokes and Belgian endive.

Ragoût of Lamb with Savory Rice

½ leg of lamb (shank or butt half), boned but with the bones
3 tablespoons butter
2 onions, thinly sliced
1 clove of garlic, crushed
1 tablespoon paprika
1 tablespoon flour
1 teaspoon tomato paste
½ cup white wine, or dry vermouth (optional)
1½ cups stock
salt and pepper
bouquet garni, or pinch of mixed herbs (thyme, basil, rosemary)

For savory rice
¾ cup rice
4 slices of bacon, diced
2 tablespoons butter
1 cup (¼ lb) mushrooms, sliced
package of frozen peas, or 1 cup cooked peas
4 medium tomatoes, peeled, seeded and cut in 8 pieces

If white wine is not available, white vermouth is a good substitute. Otherwise use ½ cup extra stock.

Method

Make a well-flavored stock with the lamb bones. Cut meat in 2 inch cubes, leaving a little fat. Heat butter in a flameproof casserole and, when foaming, add meat. Fry briskly until meat is just brown, turning occasionally. Keep the heat slightly lower for lamb than for beef.

Take out meat and keep hot. Add onions and garlic to casserole and cook over medium heat for 4–5 minutes until soft, stirring occasionally. Add paprika and flour, cook 1 minute and stir in tomato paste, wine and stock. Bring to a boil, season, and add meat with bouquet garni. Cover tightly and simmer on top of stove or in a moderately low oven (325°F) for 1½ hours or until meat is tender.

For savory rice: boil rice in plenty of salted water for 10—12 minutes or until cooked. Drain in a colander, rinse with hot water and make drainage holes with a spoon handle. Leave 30 minutes.

In a large frying pan or skillet fry the bacon for 1—2 minutes, then add the mushrooms. Fry gently for 4—5 minutes until bacon is brown, then add rice, peas and tomatoes. Season well and toss with a fork over brisk heat for 2 minutes until thoroughly hot. Transfer to a serving dish. Remove bouquet garni and serve lamb in its casserole or transfer to a serving dish.

Navarin of Lamb

2½—3 lb neck, or riblets, of lamb
1½ tablespoons meat drippings or oil
2 carrots, cut in strips
1 large turnip, cut in 8 pieces
2 onions, quartered
pinch of sugar (optional)
1 tablespoon flour
2 cups stock, or water
salt and pepper
bouquet garni

Method
Trim meat, leaving a little fat. Heat drippings or oil in a skillet or a shallow flameproof casserole, add meat a few pieces at a time and brown on both sides. Take out and keep warm. Add the vegetables and fry more slowly until they are just browned. A good pinch of sugar may be added to help browning.

Stir in the flour, cook 1 minute and add the stock or water. Bring to a boil, stirring, and replace the meat. Make sure the liquid comes just level with the meat. Season, add bouquet garni, cover casserole and simmer gently for 1½ hours or until meat is tender, turning the pieces from time to time. Remove bouquet garni and serve with mashed potatoes.

Navarin is named for the Greek town of Navarino where the decisive battle for Greek independence was fought in 1827. Navarin normally refers to a lamb stew cooked with root vegetables and a recipe for this type of stew was written in 1830 by the French Chef Carême, who liked to name his recipes for battles.

Irish Stew

2½—3 lb neck of lamb
4 medium onions
4 medium potatoes
salt and pepper
2 cups water

In the days of large households a forequarter of lamb would be used to make this dish, which combines the staple foods of the old Irish kitchens. Like most stews, Irish stew reheats well, but must be brought to boiling point before serving.

Method
Trim sinew and most of the fat from meat. Cut it into large chunks. Peel and quarter or slice onions; peel and slice potatoes thickly, or cut them in chunks.

Arrange meat and vegetables in a casserole in layers, starting and finishing with potatoes. Season well between each layer. Add the water to the pan, cover tightly and cook in a moderately low oven (325°F) for 2 hours or until meat is very tender and gravy thick and rich. Avoid stirring, but take the casserole out and shake it from time to time so the stew does not stick. Transfer to another dish, or serve in the casserole.
Watchpoint: long, slow cooking is essential for Irish stew so that the gravy is thickened and enriched by the potato and onion, which cook down to a purée.

Chicken Fricassée

3½—4 lb roasting chicken or fowl
1 onion, quartered
1 carrot, quartered
2 stalks of celery
6 peppercorns
bouquet garni
salt
velouté sauce, made with
    2 tablespoons butter,
    2 tablespoons flour, 1½ cups chicken stock (see method),
    2 egg yolks, ¼ cup heavy cream, pinch of nutmeg

For devil mixture
3 tablespoons butter
1 teaspoon Worcestershire sauce
1 teaspoon prepared mustard
¼ teaspoon cayenne

For garnish
4 medium tomatoes, halved
1 tablespoons chopped parsley

In this recipe, the dark meat is deviled to provide a contrast with the white meat and rich sauce.

Method
Put the whole bird in a kettle with the vegetables, peppercorns, bouquet garni, a little salt and water to cover. Cover pan and simmer 45 minutes—1 hour for the roasting chicken, or about 1½ hours for the fowl, or until the bird is tender and no pink juice runs out when thigh is pierced with a fork.

Lift out the bird and reserve it. Boil the stock until it is reduced to 1½ cups, strain it and reserve.

Cut legs and thighs from the bird, cut each leg in half, discarding the skin, and score the surface of the meat. Cut the breast and wing meat into strips, discarding skin and bones.

To make the devil mixture: melt 1 tablespoon butter, add Worcestershire sauce, mustard and cayenne, and spoon the mixture over the chicken legs. Let stand at least 1 hour, turning the pieces from time to time.

Make the velouté sauce (see Volume 2), using the strained stock. Simmer 2—3 minutes or until the sauce is the consistency of heavy cream. Mix the egg yolk and cream liaison in a bowl, stir in a little of the hot sauce and stir this mixture back into the remaining sauce. Heat gently, stirring, until the sauce thickens slightly; do not boil or it will curdle.

Add the nutmeg, season to taste and add the white chicken meat. Cover and heat in a water bath for 10—15 minutes or until very hot.

To finish the devil mixture: melt the remaining butter and fry the chicken legs over medium heat on all sides until golden brown. Take out, arrange on a platter, spoon the white chicken sauce mixture down other side and keep hot.

To prepare the garnish: fry the tomato halves in the pan over high heat until browned and just cooked, season lightly and arrange on the platter. Sprinkle with parsley just before serving.

Beef stew is one of the simplest and most appetizing stews to make

Beef Stew

2 lb chuck or round steak
2 tablespoons oil
3 medium onions, quartered
3 carrots, quartered
4 stalks of celery, cut in 2 inch
   sticks
1 tablespoon flour
2–3 cups beef stock
1 teaspoon tomato paste
bouquet garni
salt and pepper

Method

Cut beef into 2 inch cubes. In a flameproof casserole heat oil and, over high heat, brown the beef on all sides, a few pieces at a time. Take out beef, add onions, carrots and celery, lower heat and cook 10 minutes or until lightly browned. Pour off any excess fat, stir in flour and cook 2–3 minutes or until brown. Pour on 2 cups stock and bring mixture to a boil, stirring.

Replace meat, add tomato paste, bouquet garni and salt and pepper to taste. The stock should almost cover the beef, so add more if necessary. Cover and simmer gently on top of the stove or in a moderately low oven (325°F) for 2 hours or until beef is very tender. Stir stew occasionally during cooking and add more stock to keep the beef almost covered — the sauce should reduce a little during cooking, but the meat must not become dry.

When cooked, remove bouquet garni, taste gravy for seasoning and serve with mashed or boiled potatoes.

Paprika Goulash

1½ lb chuck or round steak
2 tablespoons oil or meat
   drippings
1½ cups sliced onions
1 tablespoon paprika
1 tablespoon flour
2 teaspoons tomato paste
2–2½ cups beef stock
bouquet garni
1 clove of garlic, crushed
salt and pepper
1 red or green pepper, cored,
   seeded and sliced
2 tomatoes, peeled, seeded and
   cut in 8 pieces
¼ cup sour cream (optional)

Method

Cut the meat in large cubes, brown them quickly in a flameproof casserole or Dutch oven in the hot oil or drippings; remove. Lower heat, add onions and cook 3–4 minutes. Stir in paprika, cook slowly for 1 minute and add flour, tomato paste and stock. Stir until boiling, replace meat, add bouquet garni, garlic and seasoning. Cover and simmer on top of the stove or in a moderately low oven (325°F) for 2 hours or until meat is tender.

Blanch the pepper, drain and refresh under cold water. Add to goulash with the tomato pieces. Bring slowly to a boil; transfer to a serving dish after removing the bouquet garni. If you like, stir in the sour cream lightly so the sauce looks marbled. Serve with boiled potatoes or noodles.

Ragoût of Beef with Madeira

1½–2 lb chuck or round steak
¼ cup Madeira
2 tablespoons oil
16–18 baby onions, peeled
1 tablespoon flour
2 cups stock
bouquet garni
1 clove of garlic, crushed
salt and pepper
2 cups (½ lb) mushrooms,
   quartered
1 cup green olives, pitted

Method

Cut the beef into 2 inch cubes. Heat the oil in a thick, flameproof casserole and brown the beef, a few pieces at a time. Take out the beef, turn down the heat and brown the onions also. Take out the onions and reserve them. Discard all but 1 tablespoon oil.

Replace the beef, stir in the flour and cook ½ minute. Pour in the Madeira, heat until nearly boiling and flame it. Add the stock, bouquet garni, garlic and seasoning, cover pot and simmer gently for 1½ hours or until the beef is almost tender. Add the onions and mushrooms and cook 15 minutes longer or until the beef and vegetables are tender.

Add the olives and heat thoroughly. Discard bouquet garni, taste the stew for seasoning and serve with buttered noodles or pasta shells.

Ragoût of Beef with Celery and Walnuts

1½ lb chuck or flank steak
2 tablespoons bacon fat, or
   drippings
12 small onions, peeled
1 tablespoon flour
½ cup red wine
bouquet garni
1 clove garlic, crushed
2½ cups stock
salt and pepper
4–5 stalks of celery
1 tablespoon butter
⅓ cup walnut halves
peeled rind of ½ orange

Method

Cut beef in 2 inch cubes. Heat fat in a thick, flameproof casserole, add beef and fry until brown, turning once. Take out meat, add onions and fry slowly until they start to brown. Take from heat and pour off excess fat, leaving 1 tablespoon. Stir in flour and add red wine, meat, bouquet garni and garlic. Barely cover with stock, season, bring slowly to a boil, cover and simmer gently for 1½–2 hours or until tender.

Cut celery in diagonal slices, discarding the leaves and tops of stalks. In a frying pan heat butter, add celery and walnuts with a pinch of salt and cook over the heat, tossing occasionally, until celery is lightly cooked but still crisp.

Cut orange rind in needle-like strips, blanch in boiling water for 5 minutes, drain and rinse in cold water. Remove bouquet garni. Transfer the ragoût to a serving dish or leave in the casserole. Just before serving, scatter celery and walnut mixture on top with the orange rind.

Goulash or gulyás is a Hungarian stew, generally of beef flavored with paprika. If lamb or pork are used, the dish may be called pörkölt. Gulyás literally means 'herdsmen's stew' and probably originated with the nomadic herdsmen's habit of cooking in a single pot over a camp fire.

Celery slices and walnut halves are cooked in butter before they are added to the cooked ragoût of beef

The finished ragoût of beef with celery and walnuts (recipe is on page 19)

Boeuf Fermière
(Beef Farmer's Wife style)

3–4 lb short ribs, short plate or shank of beef, sliced or cut in pieces
oil (for frying)
$\frac{1}{4}$ lb piece of salt pork or bacon, diced
2 tablespoons flour
1 cup red wine
1$\frac{1}{2}$ cups stock
2 cloves of garlic, crushed
bouquet garni
1 tablespoon tomato paste
salt and pepper

To finish
2 onions, chopped
3 carrots, diced
2 tablespoons butter
2 tomatoes, peeled, seeded and coarsely chopped

Method
In a thick flameproof casserole heat the oil and fry the salt pork or bacon until browned. Remove and brown the beef, a few pieces at a time, then remove and reserve.

Discard all but 2 table-spoons oil, stir in the flour and cook, stirring, until browned. Add the wine, stock, garlic, bouquet garni, tomato paste and seasoning and bring to a boil. Put back the beef, cover and simmer, stirring occasionally, for 2–3 hours, depending on the size of the pieces of meat, until the meat is tender.

If possible, make the stew a day ahead, chill it and skim off the fat that solidifies on top. If not making ahead, skim off as much fat as possible with a spoon.

To finish: a short time before serving, reheat the stew on top of the stove. Fry the onion and carrot in the butter until lightly browned, add the tomatoes and season-ing and cook 1–2 minutes longer. Taste the stew for seasoning, sprinkle the onion mixture on top and serve with mashed potatoes.

Blanquette of Veal

2$\frac{1}{2}$–3 lb breast of veal, cut in chunks, with the bone
salt and pepper
slice of lemon
2 medium carrots, quartered
2 medium onions, quartered
bouquet garni
2 cups stock, or water

For sauce
3 tablespoons butter
3 tablespoons flour
1–2 egg yolks
$\frac{1}{2}$ cup light cream
squeeze of lemon juice

Traditionally, breast of veal is used for this dish because the bones give a rich, jellied stock. However, twice as much shoulder meat as breast can be added if you like. As an alternative, breast of lamb can be substituted for veal. Meat should be well trimmed of fat, then cooked like veal breast.

For a party dish, use heavy instead of light cream in the sauce. Remove carrots and onions before serving; replace them with a mixture of 1 cup each of cooked peas, baby carrots and baby onions.

Method
Blanch veal by covering with cold water in a pan, add salt and a slice of lemon. Bring slowly to a boil, skim, drain and refresh meat in cold water to wash away the scum.

Put meat in a large kettle with carrots and onions. Add bouquet garni and pinch of salt and barely cover with stock or water. Cover and sim-mer 1–1$\frac{1}{4}$ hours until very ten-der and a bone can be pulled from meat.

Take from heat, pour off stock and reserve; remove bouquet garni. Leave meat and vegetables in the kettle, cover and keep warm. Stock should measure 2$\frac{1}{2}$ cups; if more, boil in a pan until reduced to this quantity.

To make the sauce: melt butter in a saucepan, stir in flour and cook until pale straw-colored. Take from heat; cool slightly. Stir in stock and bring to a boil, stirring constantly. Boil briskly for 3–4 minutes until sauce is creamy in consistency; take from heat.

Mix egg yolks and cream in a bowl, add a little of the hot sauce; stir mixture back into remaining sauce. Add lemon juice and taste for season-ing. Pour sauce over veal and vegetables; shake the kettle gently to mix contents together. Cover and keep hot for 15 minutes before serving to let the flavor of the sauce penetrate the meat.

Watchpoint: do not let the sauce boil or it will curdle.

Transfer to a hot dish; serve with mashed potatoes or boiled rice.

Boiled Rice

Allow $\frac{1}{4}$ cup rice per person and boil at least 3 quarts water for every cup of rice. Add salt and a slice of lemon to give flavor and whiteness.

When the water is boiling, sprinkle in the rice, stir with a fork to prevent it from stick-ing and boil steadily for 12–15 minutes or until the rice is just tender.

To stop the rice cooking, tip it at once into a colander and drain. Rinse thoroughly with hot running water to wash away any remaining starch, making several drain-ing holes in the rice with the handle of a wooden spoon.

Transfer the rice to a large tray or platter, spread it out and let stand in a warm place or in a very low oven to dry for at least 15 minutes before serving, turning occasionally with a fork.

Boeuf fermière (beef stew, farmer's wife style) tastes better when made a day ahead

Fricassée of Rabbit

4–6 pieces rabbit
2–2½ cups stock, or water (to cover meat)
2 onions, sliced
bouquet garni

For sauce
4 tablespoons butter
3 tablespoons flour
1½ cups half and half
8 (2 oz) small mushrooms

If rabbit is not available, chicken may be used instead.

The meat of a **rabbit** is fine-grained and practically all white with a mild flavor. Because of its similarities to chicken, it can be prepared in many of the same ways – fried, broiled, roasted, braised or fricasséed (as this recipe).

Rabbit is only available from good supermarkets and comes frozen, but is worth investigating for its interesting flavor.

Method
Blanch the rabbit by putting in cold water, bringing to a boil, draining and refreshing under cold water. Trim away any skin and neaten the pieces with scissors. Put rabbit into a shallow pan, barely cover with stock or water and add sliced onions.

For a more delicate flavor, first blanch the onions (put in cold water, bring to a boil and drain). Add bouquet garni, cover and simmer 1–1½ hours or until very tender. Strain off liquid and measure 2 cups.

In a saucepan melt 3 tablespoons of the butter, stir in flour and cook for half a minute. Cool a little, add liquid and bring to a boil, stirring. Boil steadily until reduced to the consistency of heavy cream. Add the half and half and bring the sauce just back to a boil.

Melt the remaining tablespoon of butter in a pan and add mushrooms. Sauté them gently until soft and add to the sauce. Transfer rabbit to an ovenproof serving dish, spoon over the sauce, cover and leave in a warm oven for 5 minutes before serving. This allows the flavor of the sauce to penetrate meat.

Blanched rabbit is cooked with stock, onions and a bouquet gar

A creamy sauce with mushrooms finishes the fricassée of rabbit

Quiche Lorraine, the most famous of the savory flans, is made with cheese, ham or bacon (recipe is on page 32)

HOW TO MAKE FLANS

Flans are open pies for which the pastry (pie pastry or the French flan pastry called pâte sucrée) is rolled out and lined into a special ring laid on a baking sheet. A flan can be filled with a sweet or savory mixture, or with fruit.

Flan rings are plain metal circles about 1 inch deep, in varying diameters. A European-type pie pan with a loose base can be used instead; these usually have a fluted edge. To avoid breaking pastry, let the flan cool before removing it from this type of pan.

Apples and pitted fruits can be baked in the uncooked pastry flan, but poached fruit and some raw fruits like strawberries should be arranged in a precooked shell. (Cooking an empty pastry shell is known as 'baking blind'.)

Once filled, all fruit flans are glazed, either with a thickened fruit juice or a jam or jelly glaze. For serving, use a flat platter or board, not a shallow dish. It is essential to chill pastry dough especially if the kitchen is hot. Chill it for about 30 minutes before rolling out to line a flan ring, and chill it again for 30 minutes before baking blind.

To line a flan ring, lift dough on rolling pin; lay over ring

Roll off excess dough after pressing dough into flan ring

Pinch around the edge to push up sides from bottom of ring

Fill paper-lined flan shell with beans before 'baking blind'

Lining a Flan Ring

Have pastry dough ready, well chilled. Set flan ring on a baking sheet, preferably without edges, so the flan can be removed easily. Roll out dough to about $\frac{1}{4}$ inch thickness, according to the recipe, and to a diameter about $1\frac{1}{2}$ inches larger than the flan ring. Lift dough on the rolling pin and lay over the flan ring, quickly easing it down onto the ring so it does not break.

With a small ball (made from dough dipped in flour) press pastry dough into the ring, especially around bottom edge.

Let dough rest over edge of flan ring and then roll the rolling pin over top of ring to cut off any excess.

Pinch around the edge with side of forefinger and thumb; then with the fingers push the dough evenly up the sides from the bottom of the ring to increase the height of the edge. Prick pastry dough base several times with a fork to release any trapped air.

Baking Blind

1 To prebake a flan shell before filling, line the flan ring with pastry dough and chill 30 minutes to set firmly.
2 Line pastry dough with crumpled foil or silicone paper, pressing it well into the dough at the bottom and sides.
3 Fill flan three-quarters full with uncooked rice or beans (to hold the shape) and bake in a preset hot oven (400°F) for 10 minutes. Turn down the heat to moderately hot (375°F) and continue baking 12–15 minutes or until the pastry is crisp and golden.
4 After baking about 15 minutes, take the flan from the oven and carefully remove the paper, and rice or beans (which may be stored in a jar and used over and over again for baking blind). Replace flan in the oven to complete cooking. The flan ring can either be removed with the paper and rice or after baking. When baked, slide the flan onto a wire rack to cool.

Points to remember

Plan to make pastry before the kitchen becomes too hot from other cooking. Work in a cool, airy room as a warm, damp atmosphere can have a disastrous result on pastry. A marble slab is ideal for rolling out dough because it is smooth, solid and cool. Use a minimum amount of flour for sprinkling when rolling, otherwise too much will go into the pastry and change the proportions. A heavy plain wooden rolling pin without handles is best, especially for puff pastry.

Be sure to clean the pastry board between rollings; any small pieces left on will stick to the dough, making it lumpy.

When baking pastry it is essential to preheat the oven to the required temperature. Immediate contact with the heat sets the pastry in its correct shape and makes it possible to estimate the baking time more accurately. See also introduction, page 27, about chilling dough before baking, especially when working in a hot kitchen.

Sweet Flans

Bakewell Flan

For rich pie pastry
1½ cups flour
pinch of salt
9 tablespoons butter
1 tablespoon sugar
1 egg yolk
2 tablespoons cold water

For filling
2 tablespoons strawberry jam
2 tablespoons lemon or orange marmelade
¼ cup butter
½ cup sugar
grated rind and juice of 1 lemon
2 eggs, slightly beaten
½ cup whole blanched almonds, ground
6 tablespoons cake crumbs

8–9 inch flan ring

Method
Make the pastry dough and chill. Roll out, line flan ring; flute or scallop the edges. Spread bottom of the dough first with jam, then with marmelade.

Set oven at moderately hot (375°F). Cream butter in a bowl, add sugar and grated lemon rind; beat until light and fluffy. Add beaten eggs, a little at a time, to butter mixture, beating constantly. Stir in almonds, cake crumbs and lemon juice. Spread almond mixture over the marmelade and bake in heated oven for 30–35 minutes or until set and golden brown.

Tarte aux Citrons (Lemon Flan)

6 lemons
¼ cup sugar
confectioners' sugar (for sprinkling)

For French flan pastry
scant 1 cup flour
¼ cup butter, softened
¼ cup sugar
2 egg yolks
½ teaspoon vanilla

For pastry cream
1 egg, separated
1 egg yolk
¼ cup sugar
2 tablespoons flour
1 tablespoon cornstarch
1½ cups milk
½ teaspoon vanilla

7–8 inch flan ring

Method
Make the pastry dough (see cherry and praline flan, Volume 2 page 14) and chill. Roll out, line the flan ring, flute or scallop the edges and bake blind for 20 minutes only, so the pastry is very lightly browned.

To make the pastry cream: beat the egg yolks and sugar until thick and light; stir in the flour and cornstarch with enough cold milk to make a smooth paste. Heat the remaining milk, stir into the

egg mixture until blended and return to the pan. Bring to a boil, stirring, and cook 2 minutes; take from the heat. Whip the egg white until it holds a stiff peak and fold it into the hot pastry cream with the vanilla. Let cool, then spread in the uncooked pastry shell.

Set oven at moderate (350°F).

Cut the rind and skin from the lemons, using a serrated-edged knife, and thickly slice the flesh. Lay the lemon slices in a skillet or heavy-based frying pan, sprinkle with sugar and cook very gently, turning once, until the slices are almost transparent.

Watchpoint: do not cook them too fast or the sugar will caramelize.

Arrange the lemon slices overlapping on top of the pastry cream and bake the flan in a heated oven for 20 minutes or until the pastry is well browned. Let the flan cool and sprinkle with confectioners' sugar just before serving.

Apple Flan Ménagère

For rich pie pastry
1½ cups flour
pinch of salt
6 tablespoons butter
2 tablespoons shortening
1 tablespoon sugar
1 egg yolk
1–2 tablespoons cold water

For filling
4–5 even-sized tart apples
sugar (for sprinkling)
¾ cup apricot jam glaze
(see Volume 1)

7–8 inch flan ring

Ménagère means 'in the style of the housewife' — homey — and this flan is one of the simplest and quickest to make.

Method
Make the pastry dough and line flan ring; flute the top edge to decorate and chill.

Pare, core, and slice the apples thinly and place at once in the flan shell, making sure that the top layer is neatly arranged in a circular pattern. Sprinkle with sugar and bake in a moderately hot oven (375°F) for 25–30 minutes or until the pastry is crisp and the apples are brown. Remove ring and cool the flan. Brush filling and pastry with apricot jam glaze.

Watchpoint: only the top layer of apple should be sprinkled with sugar as the glaze will provide enough sweetening even for very sour apples. The sugar topping helps the apple slices brown and makes them look attractive through the glaze.

If you layer the apples too thickly, or sprinkle sugar between the layers, excess juice will run out and soften the bottom of the pastry.

Peach Flan

For rich pie pastry
1½ cups flour
pinch of salt
9 tablespoons butter
1 tablespoon sugar
1 egg yolk
2 tablespoons cold water

For filling
1 lb ripe peaches, halved and pitted
1 cup water
6 tablespoons sugar
¾ cup apricot jam glaze
(see Volume 1)

7–8 inch flan ring

Method
Make pastry dough and chill.

To make filling: put water and sugar in a shallow pan, dissolve over gentle heat and boil rapidly for 2 minutes. Set aside.

Peel the halved peaches by immersing them in boiling water, leaving for 15 seconds and draining; the skins should then slip off easily. Slice the peaches.

Place the peaches in the sugar syrup, and bring slowly to a boil (this draws out the juice and increases the quantity of syrup, although the syrup will not cover the fruit at first). Simmer for about 15 minutes or until the peaches are tender. Cool in the syrup.

Roll out the pastry dough, line flan ring and bake blind. Cool on a wire rack.

Brush a light coating of apricot jam glaze over bottom and sides of pastry. Lift the peaches from the syrup and arrange in flan shell. Brush well with hot glaze. Let cool before serving.

Note: the peach syrup can be thickened and used in place of a jam glaze, but jam is better if the flan has to be kept for a while before serving.

Spiced apple flan has a topping of icing

Spiced Apple Flan

For rich pie pastry
2 cups flour
$\frac{1}{2}$ teaspoon salt
$\frac{2}{3}$ cup butter
2 teaspoons sugar
1 egg yolk
3–4 tablespoons cold water

For filling
5–6 tart apples
2 tablespoons butter
strip of lemon rind
$\frac{1}{2}$–$\frac{3}{4}$ cup dark brown sugar
$\frac{1}{2}$ teaspoon ground cinnamon
$\frac{1}{2}$ teaspoon ground allspice
$\frac{1}{4}$ teaspoon ground cloves

For icing
$\frac{1}{2}$ cup confectioners' sugar
1–2 teaspoons sherry or rum

7–8 inch flan ring

Method
Make the pastry dough and chill; line the flan ring with three-quarters of the dough. Set the oven at moderately hot (375°F).

To make the filling: wash the apples, wipe, quarter and core them. Thickly butter a heavy flameproof casserole and add the apples with the lemon rind. Cover with buttered brown paper and a lid and cook gently, stirring occasionally, until soft. Discard the lemon rind and purée the apples in a blender or work them through a nylon sieve.

Return the apple purée to the pot, add sugar to taste and spices, and cook rapidly on top of the stove, stirring constantly, or bake in heated oven until the mixture is stiff but still falls easily from a spoon. Let cool until tepid, then spread the mixture on the uncooked pastry shell. Set the oven at moderately hot (375°F).

Roll out the remaining dough, cut it in narrow strips and make a lattice on top of the flan, pressing the ends of the strips well down onto the edges of the flan to seal. Bake the flan in the heated oven for 30–35 minutes or until the pastry is browned and the filling begins to bubble. Let the flan cool.

To make the icing: sift the confectioners' sugar into a bowl and beat in enough sherry or rum to make a smooth, pourable icing. Brush the icing on top of the flan and leave to set.

Tarte Beauceronne

For rich pie pastry
1$\frac{1}{2}$ cups flour
pinch of salt
9 tablespoons butter
1 egg yolk
1 tablespoon sugar
2 tablespoons cold water

For filling
1 cup creamed cottage cheese
$\frac{1}{4}$ cup butter
$\frac{1}{4}$ cup sugar
$\frac{1}{4}$ cup seedless raisins
2 tablespoons heavy cream
3 eggs, separated
2 tablespoons flour
$\frac{1}{2}$ cup heavy cream (to serve) – optional

8 inch flan ring

Method
Make the pastry dough and chill; line flan ring. Set oven at moderately hot (375°F).

Push the cheese through a strainer and beat in a warm bowl (this helps the cheese to absorb the butter, sugar, cream and yolks without curdling and allows the egg whites to be folded in easily).

Cream the butter with the cheese, add sugar; beat until light. Stir in the raisins, cream and egg yolks until well mixed. Whip egg whites until they hold a stiff peak; fold into the cheese mixture with the flour.

Spoon filling into flan shell and bake in heated oven for 35–40 minutes or until filling is firm and brown. When baked, leave to cool in flan ring as filling rises during cooking and must be left to subside. Serve cold.

For a special occasion, top with cream, whipped until it holds a stiff peak.

Gâteau Basque

For almond pastry
6 tablespoons butter
2 tablespoons shortening
1$\frac{1}{2}$ cups flour
pinch of salt
2 tablespoons whole blanched almonds, ground
$\frac{1}{4}$ cup sugar
1 egg yolk
$\frac{1}{2}$ teaspoon vanilla
2–3 tablespoons cold water
1 egg white, slightly beaten
sugar (for sprinkling)

For filling
$\frac{3}{4}$ cup plum, or damson, jam

8 inch flan ring

Method
In a bowl rub butter and shortening into flour and salt with the fingertips, stir in the ground almonds and sugar. Mix egg yolk with vanilla and water and add to the flour mixture. Work lightly to a smooth dough and chill. Set oven at hot (400°F).

Roll out two-thirds of the dough to $\frac{1}{4}$–$\frac{3}{8}$ inch thickness and line flan ring. Fill with the jam, roll out remaining dough to a circle and lay over the top. Press down edges, mark surface with the point of a knife in a cartwheel design, cutting through to the layer of jam. Bake in a heated oven for 15 minutes, lower temperature to moderately hot (375°F) and continue baking 15–20 minutes or until the pastry is brown.

Just before the end of cooking, brush the top of the gâteau with a little beaten egg white, sprinkle with sugar and return to the oven for 2 minutes to frost the top. Serve hot or cold.

Watchpoint: the sugar must be sprinkled on the egg white quickly, before the heat of the pastry has a chance to set the white. This ensures that the sugar and egg white combine to make a meringue-like frosted topping.

Savory Flans and Quiches

Savory flans make an ideal main course for a light lunch or supper, or they can be served as an appetizer. Many of them can be prepared in advance and reheated or served cold.

A quiche is a savory flan filled with an egg custard mixture. The most famous version is quiche Lorraine, named after the district of France bordering on Germany, where quiches are thought to have originated. The word quiche is derived from the French-German dialect spoken in the region, and can be traced back to küchen, the German word for cake.

Quiche Lorraine is made with cheese, ham or bacon and sometimes with onion. Other popular fillings include crab, lobster, mushroom or ham. A quiche can be made in a flan ring, a deep pie pan or in a special pan with a fluted edge made of heatproof china, usually white.

Quiche Lorraine

For rich pie pastry
1½ cups flour
pinch of salt
6 tablespoons butter
2 tablespoons shortening
2 tablespoons cold water

For filling
2 eggs
2 egg yolks
¼ cup grated Gruyère cheese
1½ cups light cream, or milk
salt and pepper
1 tablespoon butter
4–5 slices of bacon, diced
1 medium onion, sliced, or 12 scallions, trimmed and sliced

10 inch flan ring, or quiche pan

Method
Make the pastry dough and chill; line flan ring. Set oven at moderately hot (375°F).

To make the filling: beat the eggs and the yolks in a bowl and stir in cheese and cream or milk with seasoning to taste. Melt butter in a small pan, add bacon and sliced onion or whole scallions and cook slowly until golden brown. Add to egg mixture, stir and pour into uncooked flan shell.

Bake in heated oven for 25–30 minutes or until egg mixture is set and browned.

Leek Quiche

Follow recipe for quiche Lorraine but omit bacon and onion and scallions. Substitute 4 medium leeks, well washed and thinly sliced. Fry white part of leeks in 3 tablespoons butter until soft but not browned, and add them to egg mixture; stir and pour into the uncooked flan shell.

Sausage and Tomato Flan

For rich pie pastry
1½ cups flour
pinch of salt
¼ cup butter
¼ cup shortening
2 tablespoons cold water

For filling
8 (about ¾ lb) country sausages
4 medium tomatoes, peeled and halved
2 onions, chopped
2 tablespoons butter
2 cups (½ lb) mushrooms, chopped
1 clove of garlic, crushed
1 tablespoon chopped parsley
salt and pepper
¼ cup heavy cream
oil (for brushing)

9–10 inch flan ring

Method
Make the pastry dough and chill; line the flan ring and bake blind for 20 minutes only or until the pastry is very lightly browned.

To make the filling: fry the onions in the butter until soft but not browned. Stir in the mushrooms and cook over high heat until all the moisture has evaporated. Add the garlic, parsley and seasoning and cook 1 minute longer. Take from the heat, stir in the cream and spread the mixture in the flan shell. Set the oven at moderately hot (375°F).

Fry the sausages in a little oil or broil them until they are browned. Arrange the tomato halves on the mushroom mixture with a sausage between each half. Brush the tomatoes with oil and sprinkle with seasoning.

Bake the flan in heated oven for 20 minutes or until the pastry is browned and the tomatoes are tender. Serve hot or cold.

Smoked Salmon Quiche

For rich pie pastry
1½ cups flour
pinch of salt
6 tablespoons butter
2 tablespoons shortening
2 tablespoons cold water

For filling
6 oz smoked salmon
2 eggs
2 egg yolks
1 cup heavy cream
1 cup bottled clam juice
salt
black pepper, freshly ground
½ cup grated Gruyère cheese (for topping)

9–10 inch flan ring or quiche pan

Method
Make the pastry dough and chill: line the flan ring. Set the oven at moderately hot (375°F).

To make the filling: beat the eggs and yolks in a bowl and stir in the cream, clam juice, a little salt and plenty of black pepper.
Watchpoint: if the salmon is salty, do not add more salt.

Lay the slices of smoked salmon in the uncooked pastry shell and pour in the egg mixture. Sprinkle the cheese on top and bake the quiche in heated oven for 25–30 minutes or until the egg mixture is set and browned.
Watchpoint: do not overcook or the mixture will separate.

Serve quiche hot or tepid.

Leek quiche is just one of many popular savory quiches and flans

Pissaladière

For very rich pie pastry
1½ cups flour
pinch of salt
6 tablespoons butter
2 tablespoons shortening
1 egg yolk
1 tablespoon cold water

For filling
¼ cup olive oil
4 large Bermuda onions,
    sliced
2 teaspoons Dijon-style
    mustard
6–8 medium tomatoes, peeled
    and thickly sliced
14 anchovy fillets, split
    lengthwise and soaked in
    2–3 tablespoons milk to
    remove excess salt
12–15 ripe olives, halved and
    pitted
2 teaspoons mixed herbs
    (basil, thyme, sage)
½ cup grated Gruyère cheese

9–10 inch flan ring

This flan, with its black olives and anchovy fillets, is typical of dishes from Nice on the French Mediterranean.

Method
Make the pastry dough and chill; line flan ring and chill again. Set oven at hot (400°F).

To make the filling: heat half the oil in a pan and cook onions slowly for 20 minutes or until golden. Cool. Spread mustard over bottom of uncooked pastry shell, and place onions evenly on top. Arrange tomato slices over onions and cover with a lattice of drained anchovy fillets with an olive half in each diamond. Sprinkle with the herbs and cheese and spoon over remaining oil. Bake in heated oven for 30–35 minutes or until pastry is brown.

Salé
(Swiss Cheese Pie)

For very rich pie pastry
1½ cups flour
pinch of salt
6 tablespoons butter
2 tablespoons shortening
1 egg yolk
2 tablespoons cold water

For béchamel sauce
1½ cups milk (infused with
    slice of onion, small bay leaf,
    6 peppercorns, blade of
    mace)
2 tablespoons butter
2 tablespoons flour
salt and pepper
3 tablespoons heavy cream

For filling
3 eggs
1 cup grated Gruyère cheese
pinch of nutmeg
salt and pepper

9–10 inch flan ring, or quiche pan

Method
Make the pastry dough and chill; line flan ring. Set oven at moderately hot (375°F).

Make béchamel sauce adding cream to it. When cool, beat in eggs, grated cheese and nutmeg with plenty of salt and pepper. Pour mixture into uncooked flan shell and bake in heated oven for 25 minutes or until set and brown.

Shrimp Flan

For very rich pie pastry
1½ cups flour
pinch of salt
6 tablespoons butter
2 tablespoons shortening
1 egg yolk
1 tablespoon cold water

For filling
½ lb shrimps, peeled and
    cooked
4 hard-cooked eggs, peeled
¾ cup mayonnaise
1 cucumber
salt
black pepper, freshly ground
1 tablespoon chopped dill or
    chives
6 anchovy fillets
2–3 tablespoons milk

9–10 inch flan ring, or quiche pan

Method
Make the pastry dough and chill; line flan ring and bake blind.

To make filling: cut hard-cooked eggs in half, scoop out the yolks and cut the whites in strips; combine with shrimps and mayonnaise. Push egg yolks through a sieve, cover and reserve. Peel cucumber, discarding seeds, and dice. Sprinkle lightly with salt, cover and let stand for 30 minutes. Drain, rinse, season with black pepper and add the herbs. Divide anchovy fillets in half lengthwise; soak in milk to remove excess salt.

Smoked Haddock Flan

For rich pie pastry
1½ cups flour
pinch of salt
6 tablespoons butter
2 tablespoons cold water

For filling
1½ lb smoked haddock fillet,
    cooked and flaked with
    bones removed
1 egg yolk
1½–2 cups mashed potatoes
¼ cup grated Gruyère cheese
8 scallions, chopped and
    blanched
2 hard-cooked eggs, quartered

For béchamel sauce
1½ cups milk (infused with slice
    of onion, 6 peppercorns
    blade of mace, small bay leaf)
2 tablespoons butter
2 tablespoons flour
salt and pepper

8–9 inch flan ring, or quiche pan; pastry bag and star tube (optional)

Method
Make the pastry dough and chill; line flan ring. For this recipe bake blind in a hot oven (400°F) for 20 minutes.

Beat egg yolk into mashed potato with half the cheese. Arrange flaked haddock in flan shell with scallions on top and hard-cooked eggs around edge. Make béchamel sauce and spoon over the flan.

Decorate the flan with a border of mashed potato, preferably using a pastry bag fitted with a star tube. Sprinkle the flan with remaining cheese and brown in a hot oven (425°F) for 10–15 minutes; however, if the flan was prepared ahead, reheat it for 20–30 minutes in a moderate oven (350°F) until hot and brown.

A savory flan, such as quiche Lorraine (left – recipe is on page 32) or smoked haddock flan (right), makes a very good light lunch or supper dish

White Fish Flan

For very rich pie pastry
1½ cups flour
pinch of salt
6 tablespoons butter
2 tablespoons shortening
1 egg yolk
1–2 tablespoons cold water

For filling
1 cup white fish, cooked and
    flaked with bones removed
2 tablespoons butter
2 medium onions, finely sliced
1 tablespoon flour
¾ cup milk
salt and pepper
pinch of nutmeg
2 eggs, slightly beaten
3 medium tomatoes, skinned,
    seeded and halved
2 tablespoons grated Gruyère
    cheese

8–9 inch flan ring, or quiche pan

Method
Make the pastry dough and chill; line flan ring and bake blind. Cool.

To make the filling: heat butter in a pan, add onions and cook until soft but not browned. Stir in flour and add milk. Stir mixture until boiling and simmer 2 minutes. Take from heat, season and add nutmeg. Stir in eggs.

Arrange tomatoes, cut side down, with white fish in bottom of flan shell, season well and pour over the onion sauce. Sprinkle grated cheese on top and bake in a moderately hot oven (375°F) for 20 minutes or until well set and golden brown.

Mushroom Flan

For rich pie pastry
1½ cups flour
pinch of salt
¼ cup butter
¼ cup shortening
2 tablespoons cold water

For filling
1½ cups milk (infused with
    blade of mace, small bay
    leaf, 6 peppercorns)
3 tablespoons butter
1 medium onion, thinly sliced
2 cups (½ lb) mushrooms,
    sliced
3 tablespoons flour
2 tablespoons heavy cream
    (optional)
1 egg yolk
salt and pepper
1 small egg (for glaze)

8–9 inch flan ring

Method
Make the pastry dough and chill; line flan ring, reserving about one-third to cut into strips for the top. Chill again.

Set oven at hot (400°F).

To make the filling: infuse the milk, melt half the butter in a pan, add onion and cook until soft but not browned. Add mushrooms and cook briskly over medium heat for 2–3 minutes until the moisture has evaporated. Take from heat, add the remaining butter and stir in the flour. Add milk and heat, stirring, until boiling. Simmer 3 minutes, take from heat and stir in cream, egg yolk and seasoning. Turn onto a plate to cool.

Fill the uncooked flan shell with mushroom mixture. Roll out remaining dough and cut into thin strips. Lay a diagonal lattice over top of flan, pressing ends of strips well down onto edge of flan to seal them. Cover edge with a strip of pastry dough to neaten it. Beat egg with a large pinch of salt and brush over the flan. Bake in a hot oven (400°F) for 25–35 minutes or until pastry is brown and the filling starts to bubble.

Make your menu a light buffet

Make the most of your time and your money with this menu for 12 people. For brunch or a light buffet supper serve either fricadelles — hot meatballs in tomato sauce with boiled rice — or stuffed eggs served with a colorful cold rice salad. And to finish try a griestorte with peaches — a real party dessert.

To go with your buffet food mix a Screwdriver or Bloody Mary with your own personal touch.

Stuffed Egg Salad
or
Fricadelles in Tomato Sauce

Griestorte with Peaches

Cocktail Canapé
Dried Beef Rolls

∾

Buffet Drinks
Screwdriver   Bloody Mary
Orange and Tomato Cocktail
Fresh Citrus Cocktail

TIMETABLE

Day before

For stuffed egg salad: hard-cook the eggs and make the fillings. Keep them covered in separate containers in refrigerator. Keep egg whites in a bowl of cold water in refrigerator.

Wash celery and cut; peel and slice 3 tomatoes for salad; prepare the peppers; dice and cook the carrots.

Cook rice, cool and store, covered. Make the vinaigrette dressing.

Assemble garnish; wash watercress, pick over and stand the stems in a bowl of cold water in the refrigerator.

Or for fricadelles: *make tomato sauce; prepare meatballs, roll in flour and fry.*

Drain and place in casserole; spoon over tomato sauce and bake. Refrigerate, covered ready for reheating. peel and quarter the tomatoes for garnish.

Cook rice. Drain and dry it thoroughly, and put in a buttered ovenproof dish for reheating.

Make and bake griestorte cakes. When cool, store in plastic bags.

Assemble equipment for final cooking from 10:15 a.m. for buffet lunch around 1 p.m.

Order of Work

10:15
Prepare room for entertaining: set buffet table with dishes, plates, glasses, coffee cups.

Mix all vegetables for the salad in a large bowl. Drain egg whites on a dish towel. Whip the cream and prepare the peaches; split griestortes.

Fill cakes, sprinkle with confectioners' sugar and grated chocolate and transfer to platters.

Mix rice salad and arrange on platters. Fill the eggs and garnish the platters.

11:45
Prepare your choice of soft or alcoholic drinks. Prepare coffee and keep warm.

If fricadelles and boiled rice are chosen and cooked the day before, adapt the Timetable as follows:
10:30
Start the oven at moderate (350°F).
12:30
Put the fricadelles and rice in the oven and reheat.

1:00
Serve buffet.

You will find that **cooking times** given in the individual recipes for these dishes have sometimes been adapted in the timetable to help you when cooking and serving them as a party meal.

Stuffed Egg Salad

18 eggs, hard-cooked
1 cup butter, softened
1 cup ($\frac{1}{4}$ lb) mushrooms, finely chopped
1 cup ($\frac{1}{2}$ lb) cooked chicken, without skin and bones
1 can ($7\frac{1}{2}$ oz) tuna, drained and flaked
1 package (8 oz) cream cheese
salt and pepper

For white sauce
3 tablespoons butter
3 tablespoons flour
2 cups milk
salt and pepper

For rice salad
2 cups rice
3 tomatoes
1 celery heart
1 cucumber
2 green peppers
2 red peppers
1 cup diced and cooked carrots
salt

For vinaigrette dressing
$\frac{1}{2}$ clove of garlic
3 tablespoons wine vinegar
salt
black pepper, freshly ground
$\frac{1}{2}$ teaspoon Dijon-style mustard (optional)
$\frac{1}{2}$ cup salad oil

To garnish
1 slice of canned pimiento
6 ripe olives
4 gherkin pickles
bunch of watercress
3 tomatoes

Pastry bag; $\frac{1}{2}$ inch plain tube and star tube (optional)

Method
Slice eggs in half lengthwise; remove yolks and work them through a sieve. Mix them with the softened butter, reserving 1 tablespoon for mushrooms. Keep egg whites in a bowl of cold water.

Cook mushrooms quickly in remaining butter until all moisture has evaporated. Cool and reserve. Work chicken meat through a food grinder, using the fine blade; mix with mushrooms.

To make white sauce: melt the butter and stir in the flour. Remove pan from heat and stir in the milk; return to heat and cook, stirring constantly, until the sauce thickens and boils. Boil 1–2 minutes, adjust seasoning and cover securely with plastic wrap to prevent a skin from forming on top. Cool.

Divide egg yolk and butter mixture into three parts; mix one part with chicken and mushrooms, second part with tuna, the third part with cream cheese. Add enough cold white sauce to each mixture to bind it, and season to taste.

To prepare rice salad: cook rice in plenty of boiling, salted water for about 12 minutes or until tender. Drain it in a colander, rinse in hot water to remove starch and drain again thoroughly. Transfer to a large platter, spreading it out to dry completely.

Pour boiling water over tomatoes and peel them. Cut into quarters and remove seeds; cut quarters into large strips. Wash celery heart, trim off leaves, cut heart into thin slices. Peel cucumber, dice, put on a plate and sprinkle with salt. Cover; let stand for 30 minutes to draw out excess moisture. Cut peppers in half, remove ribs and seeds; cut peppers into strips. Blanch them in boiling water for 1 minute, drain and refresh under cold running water.

To make vinaigrette dressing: crush garlic in a little bowl, and combine it with vinegar, and seasonings. Gradually beat in salad oil until dressing is emulsified.

Stuffed egg salad is garnished with peeled tomatoes, a bunch of watercress, pimiento, ripe olives and gherkin pickles

Rinse cucumber in cold water, drain and dry with paper towels. With a fork combine rice with all the vegetables, including carrots, taste for seasoning and toss with the vinaigrette dressing. Spoon a layer of the prepared rice salad onto two large dishes.

Drain and dry egg whites, and arrange firmly on the rice salad. Fill whites with the three different mixtures, using a spoon or a pastry bag fitted with a star tube for the cream cheese mixture and a plain $\frac{1}{2}$ inch tube for the other two mixtures.

To garnish: decorate chicken mixture with diamonds cut from pimiento slice, tuna mixture with half a black olive each, and cream cheese with a slice of gherkin pickle. Fill the center of each platter with a large bouquet of watercress and arrange tomatoes, peeled and quartered, or cut into eighths, around the platter.

Fricadelles in Tomato Sauce

3 lb ground veal, or 2½ lb
  ground beef mixed with
  1 lb ground pork
½ lb bacon, finely chopped
2 medium onions, finely
  chopped
1 teaspoon thyme
5 cups fresh white
  breadcrumbs
1 teaspoon paprika
1½–2 cups cold water
salt and pepper
¾ cup flour (for coating)
3 tablespoons each oil and
  butter, mixed (for frying)

For simple tomato sauce
¼ cup butter
¼ cup flour
1 tablespoon tomato paste
4 cups stock
1 can (2 lb) tomatoes
salt and pepper
1 bay leaf
1 clove of garlic, crushed

To finish
3 tablespoons heavy cream
1 cup plain yogurt
3 cups plain yogurt
3 cups rice (to accompany)
24–36 ripe olives, halved and
  pitted
2 lemons, cut in wedges

These small meatballs are an
excellent alternative to stuffed
egg salad. They can be made
from any raw, ground meat,
fried and served hot, with or
without sauce

Method
Put veal, or ground beef and
pork, and bacon in a bowl.
Add onions, thyme, bread-
crumbs and paprika. Work in
the cold water a little at a
time, kneading it in with the
hand as in bread-making.
Season well.

To prepare tomato sauce:
melt butter in a saucepan,
stir in flour until smooth and

cook until straw-colored.
Blend in tomato paste and
stock and stir until mixture
boils. Add tomatoes, crush-
ing well with the back of a
wooden spoon and stir in seasoning, bay leaf and garlic.
Cover pan and simmer 20–
30 minutes. Work mixture
through a strainer into a bowl.

Shape meat mixture into
little balls the size of walnuts,
roll them lightly in flour and
fry quickly, a few at a time,
in the hot oil and butter until
meatballs are brown. Drain on
paper towels, then lay them in
a large shallow casserole.
Spoon over tomato sauce,
cover and bake in a moderate
oven (350°F) for 30 minutes.

Before serving, mix cream
into yogurt and spoon over the
fricadelles, shaking dish gently
to mix it with sauce.

Serve with hot boiled rice.
Put black olives and wedges
of lemon in separate dishes.

Note: this dish can be prepared the day before. If you
do so, carefully transfer baked
meatballs and sauce into a
large bowl to cool as quickly
as possible. Refrigerate. Next
day replace meatballs and
their sauce in the casserole
and reheat in a moderate oven

(350°F) for 25–30 minutes so
the fricadelles are heated
through completely. While
reheating (about 10 minutes
before serving), add cream
and yogurt as described
above. As a special touch,
if you like, add 3 ripe tomatoes, peeled, quartered and
seeded, when the reheating
operation starts. The rice can
be cooked as for rice salad
(see method, stuffed egg
salad on page 38) and re-
heated in a buttered dish
covered with buttered foil in
the same oven for 20–25
minutes.

*For fricadelles, roll the meat-
balls in flour before frying*

Griestorte with Peaches

6 eggs, separated
1 cup sugar
juice and grated rind of 1 lemon
¾ cup cream of wheat
½ cup whole blanched almonds,
  finely ground

For filling
6 ripe peaches
1½–2 cups heavy cream
1 teaspoon sugar
1 teaspoon vanilla

To finish
confectioners' sugar
finely grated sweet chocolate
  (optional)

Two 8 inch cake pans

The name **griestorte** comes
from two German words —
gries meaning semolina, and
torte, a round cake or pie. In
our recipe we suggest sub-
stituting cream of wheat for
semolina because semolina
is only obtainable in specialty
stores.

This light, short-textured
cake keeps better than a
sponge cake and combines
well with fruits. These proportions give 2 cakes, each
serving 6 people.

Method
Grease the base of the cake
pans, place a circle of wax
paper in the bottom of each
pan and then grease the paper
and sides of the pans. Sprinkle
pans first with sugar and then
with flour. Set oven at
moderate (350°F).

Beat egg yolks and sugar in
a bowl for 5 minutes until
light-colored and thick. Add
lemon juice and continue
beating until thick again.
Stir in grated lemon rind,
cream of wheat and almonds.
Beat egg whites until they
hold a stiff peak and fold into

When the cakes are cold, split and fill them with stiffly whipped cream and sliced peaches

the mixture with a metal spoon. Turn into prepared pans; bake in heated oven for 45 minutes or until the cake springs back when pressed lightly with a fingertip.

If using an electric mixer, the best result is obtained by beating yolks, sugar and lemon juice together until very thick. Stir in dry ingredients as above and leave mixture standing while beating egg whites, preferably by hand with a balloon whisk. This short 'soaking time' prevents excess grittiness in the finished cake.

Watchpoint: owing to the high proportion of egg to starch, the mixture rises a great deal, then subsides. Do not open the oven door until the cake has been baking for at least 25–30 minutes.

To prepare peaches, halve them, removing pits. To peel, immerse in boiling water, leave 15 seconds and drain. The skins should slip off easily. Slice them and use at once.

Stiffly whip the cream, sweeten with sugar and flavor with vanilla to taste. When the cakes are cold, split and fill with cream and the sliced peaches. Sprinkle the tops of the cakes generously with confectioners' sugar and grated chocolate.

Cocktail Canapé for Buffet

Dried Beef Rolls

½ lb dried beef, thinly sliced
2 packages (3 oz each) cream cheese
1 tablespoon prepared horseradish (or to taste)

A canapé like dried beef rolls is ideal to serve with cocktails (see buffet drinks on page 43).

Method
Separate the slices of dried beef carefully. Spread each slice with the cream cheese mixed with the horseradish. Roll up the beef like a jelly roll and cut into pieces about 1½–2 inches in length. Fasten each little beef roll with a toothpick.

41

Simple Drinks for a Light Buffet

For cocktails at midday, few are as popular as a Screwdriver and a Bloody Mary. Despite their rather aggressive names, these drinks have a wholesome quality that makes them especially welcome and appropriate while the sun is high. And their very, bright colors bring life to any brunch or luncheon table — not to mention those guests who may have had too much of the wrong drink the night before!

Recipes for these restorative potions are almost as numerous as the enthusiasts who try them, but reduced to their essentials, they share a remarkably simple formula: part vodka to 3 parts juice — orange for a Screwdriver and tomato for Bloody Mary. Both are normally mixed with a good deal of ice and served on the rocks'.

If there is a secret to success in both these cocktails, it is the use of the freshest, highest quality juices. Since virtually all of the vodka sold here has no discernible odor or taste, the character of these drinks proceeds from their non-alcoholic ingredients. The ideal Screwdriver is mixed with freshly squeezed orange juice and the ultimate Bloody Mary is made from the pulp of home-grown tomatoes reduced to juice in a blender.

In devising your personal Screwdriver, the only other ingredient you may want to introduce is a few drops of lemon juice to hold down the sweetness. Formulae for a Bloody Mary can become much more elaborate, however, involving Tabasco and Worcestershire sauces, salt, pepper, lemon and even clam juice. It is a question of how spicy you wish to make it, but a typical cocktail for one might include a generous jigger (2 fluid oz) vodka, $\frac{3}{4}$ cup tomato juice, 2 tablespoons lemon juice and a dash each of Worcestershire sauce, Tabasco sauce, salt and pepper.

The prepared mixes for these cocktails, now widely available in grocery and liquor stores, obviously offer greater speed and simplicity. Some are quite good, particularly those for a Bloody Mary, since the positive flavor of the tomato juice and the other ingredients masks the taste of the chemical preservatives involved.

If possible, serve both cocktails to give your guests a choice and add color to your buffet table. Only one spirit is required for both drinks and the two juices could be combined in a non-alcoholic cocktail keyed to this sort of occasion and menu.

Claret Cup

2 bottles of red Bordeaux wine (claret)
$\frac{1}{4}$ cup brandy
3 tablespoons orange-flavored liqueur (Curaçao, Triple Sec, Grand Marnier)
1 orange, sliced
1½ tablespoons sugar
2–3 sprigs of fresh mint, bruised
10–12 slices of cucumber
1 teaspoon bitters
1 pint club soda
few ice cubes

Serves 10–12 people.

Method
Mix together all ingredients except soda and ice cubes in a large pitcher or punch bowl. Chill well and add soda and ice cubes just before serving.

Orange and Tomato Cocktail

2 cups fresh orange juice, strained
5 cups canned tomato juice
1 can (1 quart 14 oz) vegetable juice
3–4 sprigs of mint
rind of 1 orange, thinly peeled
pinch of salt
black pepper, freshly ground

Serves 12–15.

Method
Mix orange, tomato and vegetable juices together in a large pitcher. Bruise the mint in a little bowl and add it to the juices with orange rind. Season to taste and chill for at least 1 hour. Strain before serving.

Combine orange juice and tomato juice to make a soft-drink cocktail with a difference

Fresh Citrus Cocktail

6 cups fresh grapefruit juice
2 cups fresh lemon juice
6 cups fresh orange juice
sugar (to taste)
cracked ice

Serves 12–15.

Method
For the most flavor in fresh citrus cocktail, prepare the juices no sooner than 1 hour before serving. Just before serving, taste and add sugar, if needed, stir in cracked ice and serve in very cold cocktail glasses.

Fresh ripe fruits are one of the pleasures of the table, but their season is lamentably short. No sooner do raspberries and cherries appear in the markets than it seems they disappear. One cause of this short season is the difficulty of keeping soft, moist fruits in hot weather. Plums and apricots are relatively robust and do not deteriorate as quickly, and strawberries are usually available in most cities all year.

Since there are so many fresh fruits, we have given recipes for a selection of them; others will be included in these Volumes, together with recipes for making jams and jellies. Some of the fruits are hard to find but you can substitute — blueberries can generally be used instead of blackberries, for instance, or strawberries instead of raspberries, plums instead of apricots.

When fruit is ripe and fresh, serve it simply with sugar. Use one fruit or a mixture — like raspberries, strawberries and pitted cherries. Pick fruit over and layer it in a bowl; sprinkle each layer generously with sugar. Cover with a plate; chill for several hours before serving. By then the sugar will have melted to a rich syrup. Serve with cream and ladyfingers or a crusty-topped sponge cake.

STRAWBERRIES

Strawberries are one of the most versatile fruits and blend with flavors varying from orange and almond to cream cheese. They are even superb with a glass of red wine, in defiance of all the rules calling for sweet white wine with dessert.

Freshly picked ripe strawberries have a fragrance all their own; they can be served simply with cream or elegantly in a brandy syrup. Winter is the time to dress them up as a mousse or gâteau, when they have been picked several days before appearing in the market. When necessary you can substitute strawberries frozen without sugar for fresh ones — their flavor is good, although they will be soft and moist in texture.

Strawberries Romanoff

1 pint strawberries
1 orange
2 tablespoons sugar
1 cup heavy cream

Method
Hull strawberries and halve or lightly crush them. Grate orange rind on finest side of grater, taking care not to remove any white pith. Squeeze the juice from half the orange and combine it in a small bowl with the sugar and rind. Stir with a wooden spoon until the sugar dissolves. Whip the cream until it holds a soft shape and stir in the orange syrup. Fold this cream into the strawberries, pile in a bowl, cover and chill 30 minutes before serving.

French, not Russian, food was invariably served at the court of Imperial Russia and **strawberries Romanoff**, although a typically French dish, is named for the royal family of Russia. Sometimes the whipped cream is flavored with Curaçao liqueur as well as orange juice.

Strawberries with Orange

1 quart strawberries
6–8 cubes of sugar
1 large orange
$\frac{1}{4}$ cup brandy

Method
Hull strawberries and place in a bowl. Rub the sugar cubes over the rind of the orange until they are soaked with the oil, then crush them. Squeeze juice from the orange and combine it with crushed sugar and brandy. Stir until the sugar is dissolved and pour over the strawberries. Cover and chill thoroughly for 2–3 hours before serving.

Strawberries with Macaroons

1 pint of strawberries
3 large macaroons, broken in pieces
grated rind and juice of 1 orange
1–2 tablespoons sugar
$\frac{3}{4}$ cup heavy cream

Method
Hull strawberries and layer them in a bowl with the macaroon pieces. Moisten with half the orange juice. In another bowl combine remaining juice with the orange rind and sugar and stir until the sugar is dissolved. Whip the cream until it holds a stiff peak, stir in the orange syrup and pile it on top of the strawberries. Chill 1 hour before serving.

Strawberries in Raspberry Cream

1 pint strawberries
$\frac{1}{2}$ pint fresh raspberries, or 1 package frozen raspberries
granulated sugar (for sprinkling)
juice of $\frac{1}{2}$ orange
1–2 tablespoons kirsch
$\frac{1}{4}$ cup confectioners' sugar
$1\frac{1}{2}$ cups heavy cream

Method
Hull strawberries, place them in a bowl, sprinkle with granulated sugar to taste (less will be needed if frozen raspberries are used in the cream) and spoon over the orange juice and kirsch. Cover and chill.

To prepare the raspberry cream: push the raspberries through a nylon sieve or purée them in a blender and strain to remove the seeds. Beat in the confectioners' sugar a little at time. Whip the cream until it holds a soft shape, carefully fold in the raspberry purée and spoon this over the strawberries.

Strawberry Flan

For French flan pastry
scant 1 cup flour
½ cup butter, softened
½ cup sugar
3 egg yolks
½ teaspoon vanilla

For filling
1 pint strawberries, hulled
1 cup red currant jelly glaze

7–8 inch flan ring

Method
First prepare pastry dough: sift the flour onto a board or marble slab and make a large well in the center. Add butter, sugar, egg yolks and vanilla and work together with the fingertips until smooth. Gradually draw in flour, working with the whole hand to form a smooth dough. Chill 1 hour, roll out and line the flan ring; bake blind in a moderately hot oven (375°F) for 20–25 minutes or until the pastry is lightly browned.

When the flan shell is cool, fill with strawberries, arranging them in circles, and brush with the hot glaze, allowing it to run down between the strawberries. Leave the glaze to set before serving.

Strawberry Galette

1 pint strawberries, hulled
2 eggs
6 tablespoons sugar
½ cup flour
pinch of salt
grated rind of ½ lemon
1 cup glacé icing (to finish)

For syrup
¼ cup sugar
5 tablespoons water
1–2 tablespoons Maraschino, or Curaçao, liqueur

7 inch cake pan

Method
Set oven at moderate (350°F) and lightly grease the pan.

Beat eggs and sugar in a bowl over a pan of hot water with a rotary beater until the mixture is thick and leaves a ribbon trail when the beater is lifted. Take from heat and beat until cold. If using an electric beater, no heat is necessary. Sift flour with salt, fold into mixture in three portions with lemon rind and pour into prepared pan. Bake in heated oven for 20–25 minutes or until cake springs back when pressed lightly with a fingertip.

Cut strawberries into thick slices. For the syrup, dissolve sugar in water, and boil until syrup will spin a thread between finger and thumb when a little is lifted on a spoon (230°F–234°F on a sugar thermometer). Cool, stir in the liqueur, pour over the strawberries and let macerate 15–20 minutes.

Split cake into two layers, drain strawberries and arrange them on bottom layer. Spoon over some of the syrup, replace top layer and spoon over remaining syrup. Coat cake with icing about 30 minutes before serving.

Strawberry Shortcake

1 pint strawberries, hulled
2 cups flour
10 tablespoons butter
¾ cup confectioners' sugar
2 egg yolks
1 teaspoon vanilla
1 cup heavy cream
sugar (to taste)
confectioners' sugar (for sprinkling)

Pastry bag and medium star tube

Method
Sift flour onto a board or marble slab, make a well in the center and add butter, confectioners' sugar, the egg yolks and ½ teaspoon vanilla. Mix these ingredients with the fingertips, then draw in flour and work to a smooth dough. Chill 1 hour.

Set oven at moderate (350°F). Divide dough in two, roll or pat out into two 9 inch rounds about ¼ inch thick and place on a baking sheet. Bake in heated oven for 15–20 minutes or until cream colored. Trim shortcake to neat circles while warm and cut one into 8 sections. Cool on a wire rack.

Slice strawberries, reserving 8 for decoration. Whip cream until it holds a soft shape, beat in remaining vanilla with sugar to taste and continue beating until stiff; reserve one-third for decoration. Combine sliced strawberries with remaining cream.

Spread cream and fruit on the plain round of shortcake, smooth over and arrange the sections of shortcake on top. Sprinkle with confectioners' sugar and decorate with rosettes of cream and the reserved strawberries.

Red Currant Jelly Glaze
Whisk ¾ cup jelly until it liquefies. Rub it through a strainer into a saucepan. Heat the jelly gently, without stirring, until it is clear (boiling spoils its color and flavor).

Glacé Icing
For about 1 cup: put 3 cups sifted confectioners' sugar in a bowl, stir in strained juice of ½ orange and enough water (added 1 teaspoon at a time) to make a thick paste. Stand icing bowl in a saucepan of hot water or use a double boiler; be sure the mixture does not get too hot. If necessary, add a little more water to thin the icing until it just coats the back of a spoon. Pour over the cake or galette and spread quickly with a metal spatula.

A mouth-watering slice of strawberry walnut cream cake

Strawberry Walnut Cream Cake

4 eggs
½ cup sugar
1 tablespoon instant coffee
¾ cup flour
½ cup finely chopped walnuts

For filling
1 pint strawberries, hulled
1 cup heavy cream

8 inch springform pan

Method
Grease the pan and sprinkle first with granulated sugar, then with flour. Set oven at moderate (350°F).

To prepare the cake: beat the eggs and sugar with instant coffee over a pan of hot water, with a rotary beater until the mixture is thick and leaves a ribbon trail when the beater is lifted. Take from heat and beat until cool. If using an electric beater, no heat is necessary. Sift flour and fold into egg mixture in 3 portions with the walnuts. Turn into prepared pan and bake in the heated oven for 30—35 minutes or until cake springs back when lightly pressed with a fingertip.

Turn cake onto a wire rack to cool. Slice strawberries (reserve a few whole ones for decoration). Whip the cream until it holds a soft shape. When cake is cold, split in 3 layers and fill with two-thirds of the whipped cream mixed with the sliced strawberries. The filling should be really lavish. Spread remaining cream on top of cake and decorate with reserved strawberries.

Strawberry Tabatières

½ pint strawberries, hulled
½ cup red currant jelly glaze (see page 47)
1 cup heavy cream

For choux pastry
6 tablespoons butter
1 cup water
1 cup flour, sifted
4 eggs

For pastry cream
1 egg, separated
1 egg yolk
¼ cup sugar
½ teaspoon vanilla
2 tablespoons flour
1 tablespoon cornstarch
1¼ cups milk

For praline
⅓ cup whole unblanched almonds
¼ cup sugar

Pastry bag and ⅜ inch plain tube

Method
Set oven at hot (400°F).

First make choux pastry: bring butter and water just to a rolling boil, take from heat and, when bubbles have subsided, tip in the flour all at once. Beat mixture vigorously until smooth. Cool slightly, then thoroughly beat in eggs one at a time (this may be done using an electric mixer). Dough should be smooth, glossy and of a consistency that will just drop from the spoon. Put dough into a pastry bag fitted with a three-eighths inch plain tube and pipe small turnover shapes onto a damp baking sheet. Bake in the pre-heated oven for 20 minutes, or until pastry is brown and very crisp.

To prepare pastry cream: beat egg yolks, sugar and vanilla until thick and light; stir in flour and cornstarch with enough cold milk to make a smooth paste. Heat remaining milk, stir into egg mixture until blended; return to pan. Bring to a boil, stirring, and take from heat. Whip egg white until it forms a stiff peak.

In a bowl, fold one-third of the pastry cream into the egg white. Add this mixture to pan with remaining pastry cream and stir gently over heat for 2—3 minutes to cook the egg white. Turn into a bowl and cool. Make praline (see box on page 51).

Whip cream until it holds a soft shape and fold into pastry cream, adding enough praline to flavor it well.

Cut choux pastry turnovers in half and fill them with praline cream. Replace tops. Dip into or brush strawberries with warm red currant jelly glaze, halving them if they are large, and place around edge of each 'tabatière'. Arrange on a platter to serve.

> **Tabatière** is the French word for a snuff box, snuff being 'tabac (tobacco) à riose'. This recipe takes its name from the choux pastry piped into a turnover shape like a tobacco pouch.

Tartelettes Cœur à la Crème

1 cup quantity of French flan pastry (see strawberry flan recipe, page 47)

For filling
½ pint small ripe strawberries, hulled
1 package (3 oz) cream cheese
sugar (to taste)
¼ cup heavy cream
¾ cup red currant jelly glaze (see box, page 47)

6—8 tartlet pans

To make the classic **cœur à la crème**, curd cheese is mixed with a little fresh heavy cream (plain or lightly whipped). This is then put into small heart-shaped wicker baskets lined with cheese-cloth and left to drain for about 12 hours. When turned out the little hearts are served with light cream and sugared fruit.

Method
Prepare pastry dough and chill 1 hour. Set oven at moderately hot (375°F). Roll out dough thinly and line tartlet pans. Prick bottoms and bake blind in heated oven for 10—12 minutes or until lightly browned.

Soften cheese by pushing it through a sieve, add sugar to taste and beat in the cream.

When pastry shells are cold, fill them with cheese mixture and cover with strawberries. Brush warm red currant jelly glaze over the strawberries. Leave to set before serving.

CHERRIES

Americans may have exclusive rights on cherry pie, but cherries are held in high esteem from Tokyo to Turkey (where the fruit is believed to have originated). There are two types: sweet red or pink eating cherries, and the deep red sour or tart cherries that are used in pies and for making compotes, or served as a garnish with savory dishes.

Sweet red cherries are widely available June through July, but tart cherries are another matter. Away from growing areas, few reach the retail market as they are snapped up for canning by commercial firms. Acceptable as a substitute are cherries canned in water or light syrup.

Pink or light-colored cherries are equally hard to find as most of them are preserved in Maraschino liqueur for cocktails. They are much more common in Europe, where they are often called for in recipes like the gâteau Bigarreau on page 52. (The Bigarreau is the finest of the light-colored varieties of cherry).

Pitting Cherries
There are special gadgets for pitting cherries, but the best and simplest implement is a small, pea-sized vegetable scoop. Alternatively, try the point of a potato peeler or the bend of a hairpin. Insert the tool at the stem hole, give a twist and draw out the pit.

Rich cherry compote is delicious as an accompaniment to pork and poultry, or with cream dessert

Rich Cherry Compote

1½ lb fresh or 1 can (16 oz) tart or dark red sweet cherries
1 tablespoon sugar
pinch of ground cinnamon
½ cup red wine
2–3 tablespoons red currant jelly
grated rind and juice of 1 orange
2–3 teaspoons arrowroot, or cornstarch (mixed to a paste with 2 tablespoons water) – optional

This may be served hot or cold with pork and poultry dishes, or with cream desserts.

Method
Pit the fresh cherries; combine them in a saucepan with the sugar and cinnamon. Cover and heat until the juice runs from the cherries (almost at boiling point); turn them into a bowl. If using canned cherries, there is no need to boil them.

In a saucepan boil wine to reduce by half and stir in jelly, orange rind and juice; heat gently until jelly is melted. Strain the juice from fresh cherries or use the liquid from the can; add 2 teaspoons arrowroot or cornstarch paste.
Watchpoint: if preferred, the arrowroot or cornstarch paste may be omitted, but it does help to bind the liquid together.

Bring the liquid to a boil, stirring. If using arrowroot, remove pan as soon as the liquid thickens; cool cornstarch 2 minutes longer. Take pan from heat and add the cherries.

Cherry Mousse

1½ lb fresh Bing cherries or 2 cans (16 oz each) Queen Anne or dark sweet cherries, drained and pitted
1½ envelopes gelatin
¾ cup sugar
¾ cup water
2 tablespoons kirsch
1½ cups heavy cream

Ring mold (5 cup capacity); pastry bag and medium star tube

Method
Lightly oil the mold.
Purée the cherries in a blender or work them through a food mill — there should be 2 cups purée.

Sprinkle the gelatin over ¼ cup of the water and let stand 5 minutes until spongy

In a pan heat the sugar with the remaining ½ cup water until dissolved, then boil until the syrup forms a thread between finger and thumb when a little is lifted on a spoon (230°F–234°F on a sugar thermometer). Let the syrup cool a little, then stir it into the gelatin until dissolved. Stir the gelatin mixture into the cherry purée with the kirsch.

Whip 1 cup of cream until it holds a soft shape. Chill the cherry mixture in the refrigerator or over a bowl of ice, stirring occasionally, until the mixture starts to set. At once fold in the whipped cream. Pour the mixture into the ring mold, cover tightly and chill at least 2 hours or until firmly set.

A short time before serving, run a knife around the edge of the mousse and pull it gently away from the mold to loosen the airlock. Turn the mold upside down on a platter and shake it gently to unmold the mousse.

Stiffly whip the remaining cream, fill it into the pastry bag fitted with the star tube and decorate the mousse with rosettes of cream.

Montmorency, a famous European variety of tart cherry, has given its name to savory dishes with a cherry garnish, as well as to this dessert.

Cherries Montmorency

compote of 1½ lb tart cherries, chilled (see left)
2 tablespoons kirsch (optional)

For orange cream
3–4 cubes sugar
1 orange
1½ cups heavy cream

For macaroons
1 cup whole blanched almonds, ground
1 cup sugar
2 egg whites
1 teaspoon vanilla, or few drops of almond extract
1 tablespoon rice flour, or all-purpose flour

Rice paper, or silicone paper; pastry bag and ⅜ inch plain tube

This is a cherry compote with orange cream and macaroons.

Method
Set oven at moderate (350°F).

To make the macaroons: work almonds and sugar well together, pounding them if preferred, to extract as much oil as possible. Break up egg whites slightly with a fork and add gradually to almond mixture, beating continuously – this may be done in a mixer. Add vanilla or almond extract with flour and leave 10 minutes. Then fill into the pastry bag fitted with the plain tube and pipe into rounds on rice, or silicone, paper spread on a baking sheet. To flatten rounds, bang sheet lightly on table. Bake in the heated oven for 12 minutes or until macaroons are golden and well cracked. Cool, peel off the silicone paper or tear away edges of rice paper, leaving the rest sticking to the macaroons (rice paper is edible).

Rub cubes of sugar over rind of orange until they are well soaked with oil. Crush them in a bowl and add strained juice of orange. Whip cream until it holds a soft shape; fold in orange syrup; continue beating until it holds a shape again.

Arrange macaroons and cherry compote, drained of juice, in a serving bowl (large macaroons may be broken in 2–3 pieces). Sprinkle macaroons with kirsch. Spoon orange cream over the top – it should be liquid enough to run over into cherry/macaroon mixture. Chill 4 hours before serving.

Plain Cherry Sauce

1 lb tart or dark sweet red cherries
2–3 tablespoons sugar
pinch of ground cinnamon
about ½ cup water
squeeze of lemon juice (optional)
2 teaspoons arrowroot (mixed to a paste with 1 tablespoon water)

This cherry sauce is good with any type of angel food or sponge cake.

Method
Pit the cherries and combine in a pan with sugar and cinnamon. Cover and set on a low heat until the juice runs freely. Remove cherries with a slotted spoon. Add water to the juice, simmer 5 minutes and take from heat. Taste for sweetness, adding more sugar if you like; if too sweet, add a little lemon juice.

Stir arrowroot paste into cherry syrup. Bring just to a boil, stirring, and take from the heat – the liquid should be the consistency of heavy cream. Add cherries to the pan; if sauce is to be served hot, reheat.

To Make Praline
Gently heat equal quantities of unblanched almonds and sugar in a small heavy pan. When the sugar is a liquid caramel, stir carefully with a metal spoon to toast nuts on all sides. Turn out into a greased pan and leave to set. When cold, crush praline with a rolling pin, or put through a rotary nut grater.

Gâteau Bigarreau

1½ lb Queen Anne or light-colored sweet cherries

For sponge cake
3 eggs
½ cup sugar
¾ cup flour, well sifted with a pinch of salt

For filling
2 tablespoons praline
½ cup heavy cream, or pastry cream (see strawberry tabatières method, page 49)

For glaze
3 tablespoons apricot jam
3 tablespoons red currant jelly
1–2 tablespoons water

For decoration
extra praline, or chopped, browned almonds

8 inch cake pan

Method
Set oven at moderate (350°F). Grease pan; line base with a circle of wax paper and grease this also. Sprinkle pan first with sugar, then with flour, discarding the excess.

To make the cake: in a bowl, beat eggs lightly with a rotary beater and gradually add sugar. Stand bowl over a pan of hot water and beat steadily until mixture is thick and leaves a ribbon trail when the beater is lifted; beat until cool. If using an electric beater, no heat is necessary. Fold in flour in 3 portions. Turn mixture into prepared pan and bake in heated oven for 25 minutes or until cake springs back when lightly pressed with a fingertip.

Meanwhile pit cherries. Put jam and jelly into a pan with water, simmer gently until smooth, then strain and cool.

Fold praline into the heavy cream, whipped until it holds a soft shape, or into the pastry cream.

When cake is cool, split it into 2 layers and sandwich the halves with praline cream. Brush the top with glaze and arrange cherries to cover top of cake. Brush top and sides again thickly with slightly warm glaze and press the extra praline or almonds around sides of cake.

BLUEBERRIES

Blueberries are one of the most plentiful of summer fruits, available everywhere June through August. Their quality is very reliable and they are generally less expensive than other berries.

To prepare them, wash under running water in a colander, shaking well so the small green berries fall through the holes. Then pick them over, removing any stalks. Cooking increases their tartness, but when uncooked they can be rather bland, so serve them with brown sugar rather than regular sugar, and sour instead of sweet cream.

Blueberry Soup

1 cup blueberries, washed
juice of ½ lemon
1 stick of cinnamon
2 cups water
pinch of salt
¼ cup sugar (or to taste)
1 tablespoon cornstarch (mixed to a paste with 2 tablespoons water)
½ cup heavy cream

In Scandinavia, this soup would be served as dessert; however, it also makes an unusually good summer appetizer, particularly when only a little sugar is added so that the flavor is tart and refreshing.

Method
Simmer blueberries, reserving a few for garnish, with lemon juice and cinnamon in water for 10 minutes or until berries are soft. Add salt with sugar to taste. Stir cornstarch paste into hot berries. Bring to a boil, stirring, and simmer 2 minutes. Take from heat, remove cinnamon and push fruit through a sieve, or purée in a blender. Cool and stir in half the cream. Stiffly whip remaining cream and garnish each bowl of soup with a spoonful of whipped cream and a few of the reserved berries.

Blueberry Muffins

1 cup blueberries, washed and dried on paper towels
2 cups flour
3 tablespoons sugar
1 tablespoon baking powder
½ teaspoon salt
1 egg
¼ cup melted butter
1 cup milk

12 muffin tins

Method
Grease muffin tins and se[t] oven at hot (425°F).

Sift flour with sugar, baking powder and salt into [a] bowl. Beat egg with butte[r] and stir into milk. Make a wel[l] in the center of the flour, add milk mixture and stir quickl[y] and lightly until just com[-] bined. Halfway through stir[-] ring, add blueberries. Th[e] batter should look lumpy. Fill prepared tins two-third[s] full of batter and bake i[n] heated oven for 25 minutes o[r] until well browned.

Hot from the oven, a blueberry muffin will brighten the morning

Blueberry Pancakes

1 cup blueberries, washed
½ cup flour
½ cup wholewheat flour
2 teaspoons baking powder
¾ teaspoon salt
¼ cup dark brown sugar
4 eggs, separated
1 cup sour cream
about ½ cup buttermilk
butter (for frying)

Method

Sift the flours, baking powder and salt into a bowl; stir in the sugar and make a well in the center. Add the egg yolks, sour cream and a little buttermilk and beat until the mixture is smooth. Beat 2 minutes, then stir in enough buttermilk to make a batter that pours easily. Whip the egg whites until they hold a stiff peak and fold into the batter with the blueberries.

Melt a little butter in a skillet or on a griddle and fry the pancakes over medium heat, turning them when bubbles rise to the surface. Serve at once with more berries and sour cream.

Blueberry Crumble

1 pint blueberries
1 tablespoon lemon juice
¼ teaspoon ground cinnamon
¼ teaspoon ground allspice
½ cup butter
1 cup flour
1 cup sugar
1 cup sour cream (to serve)

Method

Set oven at moderately hot (375°F).

Wash blueberries and pick them over. Place in a shallow baking dish and sprinkle with lemon juice and spices.

Cut the butter into the flour with a knife, rub with the fingertips until the mixture resembles crumbs and stir in the sugar. Spread the mixture over the blueberries and bake in heated oven for 40 minutes or until topping is crisp and brown. Serve hot or cold with sour cream.

Blueberry Condé

1 pint blueberries
3 tablespoons rice
2 cups milk
1 vanilla bean
3 tablespoons sugar
sugar (to taste)
¾ cup orange juice
1 envelope gelatin
3 tablespoons cold water
½ cup heavy cream
1 egg white
½ cup heavy cream (for decoration – optional)

Charlotte mold, or soufflé dish (1 quart capacity)

Method

Lightly oil mold or dish.

Wash the rice and simmer slowly in milk in a covered pan, with the vanilla bean for flavor, for 45 minutes or until rice is tender. Stir mixture from time to time to prevent it from sticking. Take from heat, remove vanilla bean, stir in the 3 tablespoons sugar and cool.

Wash blueberries, sprinkle with sugar to taste and add ½ cup orange juice. Chill.

Sprinkle gelatin over the water in a small pan and let stand 5 minutes until spongy. Dissolve over a pan of hot water and stir into the rice with remaining orange juice. Whip ½ cup cream until it holds a soft shape and, when mixture is cool, fold in with the egg white, beaten until it holds a stiff peak.

Pour mixture into the mold or dish and chill 2–3 hours or until set. Just before serving, turn onto a platter and surround with blueberries. Whip cream for decoration and cover top of mold with it, if you like.

Condé, the title of an old French family, is the name given to a molded rice cream. It is also often used to describe a sweet dish featuring rice.

Cinnamon Flan
(Tarte Cannelle)

1 pint blueberries
3–4 tablespoons sugar
sugar (for sprinkling)

For French flan pastry
1¼ cups flour, sifted with
  2 teaspoons ground cinnamon
6 tablespoons butter
6 tablespoons sugar
3 egg yolks

8 inch flan ring

Method

Make the pastry dough (see strawberry flan method, page 47) and chill 1 hour. Wash and pick over blueberries and put in a large pan with sugar. Stir over low heat until juice begins to run, then cook more rapidly until mixture is thick and rich-looking. Spread onto a plate to cool.

Set oven at hot (400°F). Roll out dough, line flan ring, pushing the sides well up, prick the base and chill. Fill with cold blueberry mixture. Roll out pastry trimmings, cut in strips and lay them in a lattice pattern over the flan. Put one strip around edge of flan, pressing it down firmly. Brush dough lightly with water and sprinkle with sugar.

Bake in heated oven for 10 minutes, lower heat to moderately hot (375°F) and continue baking for 12–15 minutes or until pastry is brown and crisp. Serve flan while still warm – the French call this 'chambré' (room temperature).

RASPBERRIES

Berries deteriorate quickly, but raspberries suffer the most because they may mold within 24 hours of picking. This makes them scarce and expensive, but red raspberries remain a favorite, whatever their price. Be sure to use them in recipes where their flavor is not overwhelmed by other strong ingredients. Black raspberries can be used in all red raspberry recipes, although their flavor is not as distinctive.

Raspberries in Melba Sauce

1 quart raspberries
¼ cup confectioners' sugar

Method

Purée one-third of the raspberries by pushing them through a sieve, or puréeing them in a blender, then straining to remove the seeds. Sift sugar and beat into purée a little at a time. Pour this sauce over remaining raspberries in a serving bowl and chill at least 1 hour before serving.

Serve Linzer torte cold as a dessert or at a coffee party

Crème Suisse

6 Petit Suisse cheeses, or
$\frac{3}{4}$ cup cream cheese
4 eggs, separated
4—6 tablespoons sugar
$\frac{3}{4}$ cup heavy cream
$\frac{1}{4}$ cup Grand Marnier

To serve
1 quart fresh raspberries,
sprinkled with sugar, or
raspberries in Melba sauce

Method
Beat egg yolks with sugar until thick and light. Beat in cream cheese, cream and Grand Marnier. Whip egg whites until they hold a stiff peak; fold into mixture. Cover and freeze for 2 hours. Spoon cream into a chilled bowl; serve with raspberries sprinkled with sugar or raspberries in Melba sauce.

Linzer Torte

2 cups flour
pinch of salt
$\frac{1}{2}$ teaspoon ground cinnamon
$\frac{1}{2}$ cup butter
$\frac{1}{2}$ cup sugar
1 egg
1 egg yolk
grated rind of 1 lemon
$\frac{2}{3}$ cup whole unblanched
almonds, ground

For filling
1 quart fresh raspberries, or
2 packages frozen
raspberries, drained
sugar (to taste—for fresh
raspberries)

To finish
$\frac{3}{4}$ cup red currant, or raspberry,
jelly glaze (see page 47)

7 inch flan ring

If using frozen raspberries, drain thoroughly by standing them in a nylon strainer for at least 15 minutes.

Method
In a saucepan bring raspberries rapidly to a boil, adding sugar to taste to fresh ones, and cook 2—3 minutes. Cool.

Sift flour with salt and cinnamon onto a board or marble slab. Make a well in the center and add butter, sugar, eggs and lemon rind. Sprinkle ground almonds on the flour. Work these ingredients together into a smooth dough and chill 1 hour.

Set oven at moderately hot (375°F). Roll out dough to $\frac{1}{4}$—$\frac{1}{2}$ inch thickness and line flan ring, keeping the trimmings. Fill with cold raspberry mixture. Arrange a lattice of strips made from the trimmings across top and bake in heated oven for 25 minutes or until pastry is beginning to brown. Cool and brush torte with red currant or raspberry jelly glaze.

Blackberry summer pudding is a traditional English fruit dessert

BLACKBERRIES

Today's wild crops are fewer and fewer, but somehow blackberries manage to survive almost anywhere and it is still possible to pick a generous basket of wild blackberries in many country areas. The height of the season is in June and July and there are few better ways to enjoy these berries than in the traditional English summer puddings.

Summer Pudding 1

1 quart blackberries, red or black raspberries, loganberries, or black currants, cleaned
½ cup water
sugar (to taste)
10—12 slices of white bread
1 teaspoon arrowroot, or cornstarch (mixed to a paste with 1 tablespoon water)
1 cup heavy cream (to serve)

Deep bowl, or soufflé dish (1½ quart capacity)

Method

Put fruit and water in a pan, cover and simmer 4—5 minutes (1—2 minutes longer for currants); strain, reserving the juice. Push fruit through a food mill or sieve, or purée in a blender, and strain to remove the seeds. Add reserved juice and sweeten well. Remove crusts from bread. Pour a little fruit purée into bottom of dish or bowl, put 1—2 slices of bread on top and add more of the purée. Continue until dish is very full, making sure each layer is well soaked with purée. Reserve a cup of purée for sauce. Put a plate and a 2lb weight on top of the pudding and leave overnight.

To make the sauce, stir cornstarch or arrowroot paste into reserved purée. Heat, stirring, until thickened; then cool. Just before serving, turn out pudding, spoon over sauce and serve with heavy cream.

Summer Pudding 2

1 quart fruit—raspberries, pitted cherries, currants, blackberries, etc., cleaned
½—¾ cup sugar
10 slices of dry white bread
1 cup heavy cream (to serve)

Deep bowl, or soufflé dish (1½ quart capacity)

Fresh bread tends to be very doughy so, if possible, use white bread left in the open air to dry thoroughly.

Method

Put fruit and sugar in a shallow pan, cover and set on a low heat for 10—15 minutes, shaking pan occasionally, until the juice has run and the fruit is tender. Cool a little and add more sugar, if you like.

Remove crusts from bread and cut 1—2 slices to fit the bottom of the bowl or dish. Arrange remaining slices around the sides, cutting them if necessary and reserving 4 slices.

Half fill the bread-lined bowl with fruit, then add a layer of bread and remaining fruit. Cover with the last slices of bread and spoon in just enough juice to fill the bowl. Put a small plate with a 2 lb weight on top and refrigerate overnight, standing the bowl on a plate to catch any juice that overflows. Turn out and serve with heavy cream.

Blackberry Bavarian

1 pint blackberries, cleaned
½ cup water
1 envelope gelatin
3 tablespoons water
sugar (to taste)

For custard
1½ cups milk
3 egg yolks
3 tablespoons sugar

For decoration
½ cup heavy cream
few whole blackberries

Ring mold (1 quart capacity), or cake pan with sloping sides; pastry bag and a medium star tube

Method

Put fruit and water in a pan, cover and simmer 4—5 minutes; strain, reserving the juice. Push fruit through a food mill or sieve, or purée in a blender and strain to remove the seeds. Add reserved juice and sweeten well.

For custard: scald milk; beat egg yolks with sugar until thick and light, stir in half the milk and return this mixture to remaining milk in the pan. Heat gently, stirring, until custard coats the back of a spoon; do not boil. Cool.

Sprinkle gelatin over 3 tablespoons water in a small pan and leave 5 minutes until spongy. Dissolve over a pan of hot water and stir into the blackberry purée with sugar to taste. Stir in custard and chill mixture, stirring from time to time, until it starts to set. Rinse mold or pan with cold water and pour in blackberry mixture. Chill 2—3 hours or until set.

Just before serving, whip the cream to a stiff peak. Turn out the mold and decorate with rosettes of whipped cream and the whole blackberries.

Blackberry and Apple Cobbler

1 pint blackberries
4 tart apples, pared, cored and sliced
about ½ cup brown or white sugar
1 tablespoon cornstarch

For topping
1 cup flour
1½ teaspoons baking powder
½ teaspoon salt
1 teaspoon sugar
¼ cup butter
about ⅓ cup heavy cream

Method

Pick over blackberries and wash them only if necessary; drain them well. Mix the blackberries, apples, sugar and cornstarch — the amount of sugar needed depends on the tartness of the apples.

Spread the fruit about 1½ inches deep in a shallow buttered baking dish. Set the oven at hot (400°F).

To make the topping: sift the flour into a bowl with the baking powder, salt and sugar. Rub in the butter with the fingertips until the mixture resembles crumbs. Stir in the cream as lightly as possible to form a rough dough.

Turn out the dough onto a floured board and roll out to cover the fruit. Lift the dough on top of the baking dish, trim the edges and bake in the heated oven for 30 minutes or until the topping is crisp and golden and the fruit is soft when tested with a skewer. Serve hot with vanilla ice cream.

CURRANTS

Currants are one of the few fruits always cooked before eating. Fresh currants have a refreshing tangy flavor that is quite unmistakable; however, as most of the crop is bought by commercial firms, few find their way to retail markets. Cultivation of currants is illegal in some states because bushes harbor a fungus which attacks the valuable white pine.

Currant Cream

1 quart fresh red, white or
    black currants
sugar (to taste)
2 egg yolks
1 egg
2 tablespoons sugar
1¼ cups milk
1 envelope gelatin
1¼ cups heavy cream
arrowroot, or cornstarch
    (mixed to a paste with a little
    water)

Charlotte mold, or soufflé dish
* (1½ quart capacity)*

Method
Lightly oil the mold or dish. Wash currants, pick them over and put in a saucepan with sugar to taste. Cover and cook over low heat for 15 minutes, or until currants are very soft. Drain them, reserving juice. Push currants through a sieve or purée in a blender. Measure 1¾ cups purée, adding enough reserved juice to make a mixture which pours easily.

Beat egg yolks with whole egg and sugar until thick and light. Scald milk; stir into egg mixture. Return to the pan and heat gently, stirring, until the custard thickens; do not

boil. Cool it.

Sprinkle gelatin over ¼ cup reserved juice in a small pan and let stand 5 minutes until spongy. Dissolve over a pan of hot water; stir into custard with the purée. Chill, stirring occasionally, until the mixture starts to set.

Watchpoint: when using an acid fruit like currants, make sure the purée is sweet enough before it is added to other ingredients or it may start to ferment if kept more than 4–5 hours.

Whip cream until it holds a soft shape, fold into custard purée mixture and pour into mold or dish. Cover and chill 2–3 hours or until set. Thicken remaining juice by heating it with arrowroot or cornstarch, allowing 1 teaspoon per cup of juice. Chill this sauce.

To serve the currant cream, turn it out onto a platter and pour around a little sauce, serving the rest separately.

GOOSEBERRIES

Really ripe gooseberries are sweet enough to eat out of hand, but tart ones are best cooked and eaten either as a compote, or puréed as in one of the following recipes. Since gooseberries are rarely available, you can use blackberries or plums instead.

Gooseberry Cream

1 quart gooseberries
4½ tablespoons sugar
1 cup water
1 envelope gelatin
green food coloring
1½ cups heavy cream

For decoration
2 cups lemon-flavored gelatine
pistachio nuts, or small
    diamonds of candied
    angelica

Charlotte, or ring, mold
* (1½ quart capacity)*

Method
Hull and wash gooseberries. Heat 3 tablespoons sugar with water until dissolved, add gooseberries and simmer 15 minutes or until tender. Drain, reserving 1½ cups syrup, and push fruit through a sieve, or purée in a blender and strain to remove the seeds.

Make lemon-flavored gelatine and cool it. Spoon half into the mold and chill until set. Arrange nuts or angelica on top and add a thin layer of gelatine; chill until set, add remaining gelatine and chill.

Sprinkle gelatin from envelope over half the reserved syrup in a small pan and let stand 5 minutes or until soft; dissolve over a pan of hot water. Stir into the gooseberry purée with the remaining 1½ tablespoons sugar and the reserved syrup, adding a few drops of green coloring. Chill, stirring from time to time, until mixture starts to set. Whip cream until it holds a soft shape and carefully fold into gooseberry mixture. Pour into mold and chill 2–3 hours or until set.

Unmold just before serving.

Gooseberry Fool

1 quart gooseberries
1½–2 cups water
sugar (to taste)
2 teaspoons orange flower
    water (optional)
1¼ cups heavy cream
ladyfingers, or crisp cookies
    (for serving)

For thick custard
1 cup milk
3 egg yolks
1 teaspoon cornstarch

Orange flower water is available in Middle Eastern markets and some pharmacies.

Method
Hull and wash gooseberries; put them in a pan with the water, cover and simmer 15 minutes or until soft. Drain, reserving the juice, and push them through a sieve, or purée in a blender, and strain to remove the seeds. Measure purée and add enough juice to make 2½ cups. Add sugar to taste with orange flower water and chill.

To make custard: scald milk; beat egg yolks with cornstarch until smooth and stir in milk. Return mixture to pan and cook, stirring, until thickened. Simmer 2 minutes and stir into the gooseberry purée. Chill.

Whip the cream until it holds a soft shape and fold into the custard mixture, leaving the fool slightly marbled with cream. Pour into a glass bowl and serve with ladyfingers or crisp cookies.

Lemon gelatine and diamonds of candied angelica make a decorative topping for gooseberry cream

COOK A COLORFUL DINNER OF CONTRASTS

Cook a colorful dinner — contrast the bland flavor of egg with piquant mayonnaise or choose a creamy soup, flavored with lettuce. The spice of curry is sweetened with peaches in the chicken entrée, while there is a choice of dessert—a rich caramel cream with a tart strawberry sauce or Crème Margot, a strawberry custard set with gelatin and decorated with rosettes of cream.

A dish with curry calls for strength of character in the wine which is to complement it. From the Rhône, birthplace of France's most heroic red wines, comes a white to meet the challenge — Hermitage. But the U.S. has a champion as well, in a wine named for the Delaware grape — by far the best of the traditional New York state whites, and its aromatic qualities and crisp taste are ideally suited to this menu.

Oeufs au Cresson
(Egg & Watercress Mayonnaise)
or
Cream of Lettuce Soup

Curried Chicken with Peaches
Boiled Rice
Cucumber Raita   *Brinjal Sambal*

Crème Caramel
with Strawberry Sauce
or
Crème Margot

White wine — Hermitage (Rhône)
or Delaware (New York)

Oeufs au cresson are garnished with lemon slices and a bunch of watercress (recipe is on page 62)

TIMETABLE

Morning

For œufs au cresson, hard-cook eggs, wash watercress and make purée from 1 bunch. Make mayonnaise. Prepare yolk mixture, cover and refrigerate. Combine watercress purée with mayonnaise, cover and refrigerate.

Or prepare lettuce soup up to the point when liaison is added. Fry cubes of bread for the croûtons in hot oil and butter until brown and crisp; drain on paper towels.

Make crème caramel, *or crème Margot*, cover and chill.

Make strawberry sauce, cover and chill.

Cook chicken; make curry sauce. Rinse out casserole, return chicken pieces and sauce to casserole and refrigerate. Cook rice, drain and dry it; put in a buttered, ovenproof dish for reheating and cover with buttered foil.

Assemble equipment for final cooking from 7.15 p.m. for dinner around 8 p.m.

Order of Work

7:15
Set oven at moderately low (325°F).

7:25
Put chicken into the oven to reheat.

Unmold crème caramel onto serving dish and pour over strawberry sauce. Refrigerate.

Stuff egg whites with yolk mixture, prepare chopped watercress with vinaigrette dressing, arrange eggs on the watercress salad bed and coat with mayonnaise.

7:45
Put rice in the oven to reheat.

Add liaison to soup and heat carefully. Warm croûtons.

Peel and slice peaches, and add them to the curry.

8:00
Serve appetizer.

You will find that **cooking times** given in the individual recipes for these dishes have sometimes been adapted in the timetable to help you when cooking and serving this menu as a party meal.

Appetizer

Oeufs au Cresson
(Egg and Watercress Mayonnaise)

4—5 hard-cooked eggs
2 tablespoons butter
½ cup mayonnaise
salt and pepper
2 bunches of watercress
squeeze of lemon juice
pinch of cayenne, or 2—3 drops of Tabasco
1—2 tablespoons vinaigrette dressing
1 lemon, sliced

Method

Cut eggs in half lengthwise, remove the yolks and work them through a sieve or strainer. Soften butter and mix it into the yolks with 1 teaspoon mayonnaise. Season with salt and pepper. Cover this mixture with plastic wrap; keep egg whites in a bowl of cold water.

Wash the watercress well and cook 1 bunch in boiling water for about 5 minutes; drain well and purée by working through a sieve or blender. Mix watercress purée with remainder of mayonnaise, a squeeze of lemon juice and the cayenne or Tabasco. Chop the second bunch of watercress coarsely, toss it with the vinaigrette dressing and spoon onto a serving dish.

Dry the egg whites, fill them with the yolk mixture and reshape. Place eggs on the chopped watercress and coat with the mayonnaise mixture. Garnish the platter with lemon slices.

Mayonnaise

2 egg yolks
¼ teaspoon salt
pinch of pepper
pinch of dry mustard
¾ cup oil
2 tablespoons wine vinegar

Makes 1 cup.

Method

In a bowl, beat the egg yolks and seasonings with a small whisk or wooden spoon until thick. Add the oil, drop by drop; when 2 tablespoons have been added, the mixture will be very thick. Stir in 1 teaspoon vinegar.

The remaining oil can be added more quickly (1 tablespoon at a time, beaten thoroughly between each addition until smooth, or in a thin steady stream if using an electric blender). When all the oil has been used, add the remaining vinegar with more seasoning to taste.

To thin and lighten mayonnaise, add a little hot water. For a coating consistency, thin with a little cream or milk.

Watchpoint: mayonnaise curdles easily so be sure to add the oil drop by drop at first, and continue adding it *very* slowly until very thick, after which you can speed up. If mayonnaise does curdle, start with a fresh yolk in another bowl and work well the seasonings. Then add the curdled mixture drop by drop. To lessen the chances of curdling, have all the ingredients at room temperature before starting.

Above: mix watercress purée into mayonnaise before seasoning it with a squeeze of lemon juice and cayenne or Tabasco

Below: place the eggs, filled with yolk and mayonnaise mixture, on the chopped watercress, tossed with vinaigrette dressing

Alternative Appetizer

Cream of Lettuce Soup

2 large heads of lettuce
2 tablespoons butter
1 medium onion, finely chopped
1½ tablespoons flour
4 cups milk
salt and pepper
1 tablespoon finely chopped mint (for garnish)
2 slices of bread, crusts removed, cubed and fried in a little oil or butter (for croûtons)

For liaison
2 egg yolks, or 1 teaspoon arrowroot
2–3 tablespoons heavy cream

Any type of lettuce — Boston, romaine, or leaf—may be used for this soup.

Method
Wash lettuce thoroughly and cut into fine shreds. In a saucepan melt butter, add lettuce and onion, cover with buttered paper and lid of pan, and cook over low heat for 8–10 minutes. Remove pan from heat and stir in the flour. Scald milk and blend it in with the lettuce mixture. Season with salt and pepper and cook, stirring constantly, until very hot. Reduce heat and simmer very gently, with lid off, for 10–15 minutes. If the soup is boiled hard it will curdle; work through a sieve or purée it in a blender.

Return soup to the rinsed saucepan and heat to a boil before adding the liaison.

For egg yolk liaison: mix egg yolks and cream in a bowl, add a little hot soup and stir this mixture into remaining soup in pan off the heat. Heat soup, stirring until it thickens, but do not boil as it will curdle. For arrowroot liaison: mix arrowroot with cream; stir into hot soup. Bring almost to a boil, stirring, until the soup thickens.

Taste for seasoning and pour into heated tureen or bowls. Sprinkle finely chopped mint on top. Serve fried croûtons in separate bowl.

Croûtons

2–3 slices of dry white bread, crusts removed
2–3 tablespoons oil
2–3 tablespoons butter

Method
Cut the bread into small cubes. In a small frying pan heat the oil and butter and add the bread — the fat should be deep enough to cover the cubes. Fry the croûtons briskly for about 30 seconds, turning them so they brown evenly. Lift them out with a slotted spoon or pour them into a wire strainer with a bowl beneath to catch the fat.

Spread the croûtons on paper towels to dry thoroughly and sprinkle them with a little salt just before serving.

If you like, fry the croûtons in advance and reheat them 1–2 minutes in a hot oven (400°F).

Serve separately.

Curried chicken with peaches is a mouth-watering entrée

Entrée

Curried Chicken with Peaches

3—3½ lb roasting chicken
2 tablespoons olive oil, or
  butter
1 medium onion, finely
  chopped
1½ tablespoons curry powder
1½ tablespoons flour
2 cups chicken stock, made
  from the giblets
1 clove of garlic, crushed
½ cup almond or coconut milk,
  (see box)
1 tablespoon red currant jelly,
  or juice of ½ lemon (mixed
  with 2 teaspoons sugar)
3—4 tablespoons heavy cream
1 teaspoon arrowroot (mixed
  to a paste with 1 tablespoon
  stock, or water) — optional
2 ripe peaches, peeled, pitted
  and sliced

To serve
1 cup rice, boiled

Method

Cut chicken into serving pieces and brown slowly in half the oil or butter in a flame-proof casserole. When brown on all sides remove from casserole and keep warm.

Heat remaining oil or butter in the casserole, add onion and cook gently until it begins to brown. Stir in the curry powder and continue cooking 2—3 minutes. Sprinkle in the flour and cook 1 minute. Remove casserole from the heat and gradually pour in the stock. Add the garlic and bring the mixture to a boil, stirring, and simmer 20 minutes.

Return chicken to the casserole, cover tightly and continue cooking on top of the stove or in a moderately low oven (325°F) for about 45 minutes or until tender. Transfer chicken to a platter and strain sauce from casserole into a pan. Add almond or coconut milk, red currant jelly or sweetened lemon juice and simmer 2—3 minutes.

Rinse out the casserole and replace the chicken pieces in it. Stir the heavy cream into the sauce and thicken, if necessary, with arrowroot paste. Spoon sauce over chicken pieces and reheat carefully (ideally on an asbestos mat), adding the peach slices 10—15 minutes before serving. Serve the chicken, with boiled rice and other accompaniments in separate dishes.

Add the sliced peaches to the chicken in curry sauce 10—15 minutes before serving

The simple curry sauce in this recipe is extremely adaptable. Obvious substitutes for the chicken are duck or turkey, but small birds like Cornish game hens, left whole or split in half, can also be used with excellent results. Cubes of veal, lamb and beef, prepared like chicken but cooked for a longer time, are an equally good base for this quick curry sauce.

Nut Milk

To make ½ cup nut milk: infuse 2 tablespoons ground almonds or dried coconut in ¾ cup boiling water for 1 hour — squeeze the mixture in cheesecloth to extract the milk.

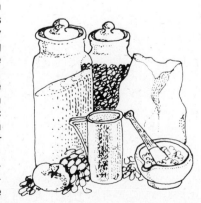

Accompaniments to entrée

Brinjal Sambal

1 medium egg plant
2 onions
3 green chilis, or 1 green bell
  pepper, cored, seeded and
  finely chopped
salt
sugar (to taste)
juice of 1 lemon
1 lime or lemon, sliced

Method

Wrap the eggplant in foil and bake in a moderate oven (350°F) for 30—40 minutes or until it is tender when pierced with a fork. Peel eggplant and crush the flesh. Mix the pulp with 1 onion, grated or finely chopped, the chilis or green pepper, salt and sugar to taste and lemon juice to sharpen the flavor.

Chill the mixture, transfer to a serving dish and garnish the top with the second onion, thinly sliced and pushed into rings, and slices of lime or lemon.

Cucumber Raita

2 cucumbers
salt
¾ cup plain yogurt
black pepper, freshly ground
sugar (to taste)

Method

Peel the cucumbers and grate them coarsely onto a plate. Sprinkle with salt, cover and let stand in the refrigerator for about 30 minutes. Then rinse the cucumber with cold water, drain well and mix in a bowl with the yogurt, black pepper and sugar to taste.

Dessert

Crème Caramel with Strawberry Sauce

For caramel
½ cup sugar
½ cup water

For crème
2 cups milk
1 tablespoon sugar
2 eggs
2–3 egg yolks

For sauce
1 pint strawberries
2–3 tablespoons sugar
(for sprinkling)

Charlotte mold, or soufflé dish (1 quart capacity)

Method

In a heavy saucepan combine sugar and ¼ cup of the water for the caramel; cook over a low heat until dissolved. Boil syrup until rich brown in color; pour in remaining ¼ cup water very carefully off the heat (caramel mixture will sizzle vigorously). Cook, stirring, until caramel is dissolved. Pour into a bowl to cool.

Set oven at moderately hot (375°F). Heat milk with 1 tablespoon sugar and stir until dissolved. Combine eggs and extra egg yolks and mix with a fork until smooth but not frothy. Stir in warm milk gradually, then add caramel mixture. Strain this custard into the lightly oiled charlotte mold or soufflé dish and cover with foil. Stand dish in a pan of hot water, bake in heated oven for 40–50 minutes, or until a knife inserted near the center comes out clean. Remove from oven and cool.

While custard bakes, hull

and cut strawberries in slices. Sprinkle them with sugar and let stand for about 30 minutes. Work berries through a sieve or purée them in a blender. Turn crème caramel from the mold onto a dish and spoon strawberry sauce over.

Below: slice the strawberries, sprinkle with sugar, and let stand before making purée

Above: pour cool caramel into warm custard mixture and stir before straining into the oiled mold or dish

Alternative Dessert

Crème Margot

1 pint strawberries (hulled and puréed, see crème caramel, left)
1 envelope gelatin
¼ cup water
½ cup heavy cream
1 egg white

For custard
3 egg yolks
3 tablespoons sugar
1¼ cups milk

For decoration
½ cup heavy cream
a few whole strawberries
a few pistachios

Glass bowl (1½ quart capacity); pastry bag and a medium star tube

Method

To make the custard: in a bowl beat the egg yolks with sugar

until light and thick. Scald the milk, add half to the egg mixture, stir well and return to the remaining milk in the pan. Heat gently, stirring, until the custard coats the back of a spoon; do not boil. Strain into a bowl and cool.

Sprinkle the gelatin over the water in a small pan and leave 5 minutes until spongy. Dissolve gelatin over a pan of hot water and stir into the custard with the strawberry purée. Place bowl over ice, and stir until the mixture starts to thicken.

Stiffly whip ½ cup cream and beat the egg white until it holds a stiff peak. Fold both into the strawberry mixture; pour into a glass bowl to set.

Whip the remaining cream and put into a pastry bag fitted with a medium star tube; decorate the crème with rosettes of cream, whole strawberries and pistachios.

Crème caramel is coated with strawberry sauce

How to Broil MEAT & FISH

A platter of broiled steaks garnished with savory butter and watercress

Broiling is quick, simple and ideal for cooks in a hurry. Broiled foods have little fat, almost no liquid and few added calories. However, broiling is expensive because the high heat used can dry out and toughen the food, and it must always be of the highest quality. Meat must be well marbled with natural fat which melts during cooking to give flavor and tenderness.

Some broiled food, like chops and kebabs, can be kept hot for a short time on the broiler rack and basted occasionally with the cooking juices, but steaks should be served at once. In general, broiled dishes are a bad choice for a dinner party because the hostess has to cook at the last minute.

Broiling needs careful attention; foods must cook at the right speed if they are to retain their juices without burning. Some, like fish or ham, must be brushed often with oil or melted butter if they are to be moist and juicy.

Turn on the broiler at least 5—6 minutes before using and leave rack and pan inside to heat. Broiling should always be done with the heat at maximum; temperature is controlled by altering the level of the broiler pan, not by reducing heat.

When charcoal broiling, the fire should be started 1 hour or so in advance. The coals should be grey and scarcely glowing when cooking begins.

Do not sprinkle salt on food before broiling as it draws out the juices and flavor is lost. Add only freshly ground black pepper and seasonings stated in the recipe. Then brush with oil (olive oil gives most flavor) or a sauce and turn over 1—2 times during cooking, keeping well basted. Season with salt at the end of cooking.

The times given for broiling are approximate as they really depend on the broiler, the thickness of the food and your personal tastes. A good guide for steak is to press it with the fingers: if it feels spongy, it is rare; if firmer and more resilient, medium rare; if firm, well done.

Plain broiled meats should be accompanied by savory butters served separately or in slices on top of steaks, chops, etc. Meats which have been brushed with barbecue sauce during cooking are usually served without a butter or sauce garnish. They look best when simply served with a bunch of watercress and French fries or baked potatoes. A green salad is a good accompaniment.

BEEF

Steak Cuts	Broiling Times			Accompaniments
Sirloin ($\frac{3}{4}$—1 inch thick, serves 2) The amount of bone varies with the part of the animal from which the steak is taken. Sirloin is a good steak for several people as it can be cut up to 2 inches thick. In such cases it should be carved in diagonal slices.	Rare: Medium: Well done:	6—7 minutes 8—10 minutes 10—12 minutes		Maître d'hôtel or garlic butter French fries or baked potatoes; fried onions; baked squash; green beans; green salad; peas.
Porterhouse ($\frac{3}{4}$—1 inch thick, serves 1) Porterhouse is a luxury cut and prices correspond. Trim it before cooking, as it can be very fat. Like sirloin, it can be cut up to 3 inches thick to serve more people.	Rare: Medium: Well done:	5 minutes 6—7 minutes 8—10 minutes		Maître d'hôtel or garlic butter sauce Bordelaise; baked or straw potatoes; sautéed cucumber; stuffed mushrooms.
Strip (1—1$\frac{1}{2}$ inches thick, serves 1) Strip or boneless loin (from the sirloin) is nothing more than a Porterhouse with fillet, and sometimes bone, removed. Known in the west as New York strip; in New York as strip steak.	Rare: Medium: Well done:	5 minutes 6—7 minutes 8—10 minutes		Boiled potatoes in their jackets or baked potatoes; French fried onion rings; fresh asparagus and lemon butter.
T-bone (1$\frac{1}{2}$—2 inches thick, serves 2) Cut from near the Porterhouse, the T-bone steak has less tenderloin and is usually slightly smaller in area.	Rare: Medium:	7—8 minutes 8—10 minutes		Maître d'hôtel or garlic butter; sauce chasseur; French fries or baked potatoes; broiled tomatoes; stuffed mushrooms.
Club or Delmonico ($\frac{3}{4}$—1 inch thick, serves 1) This steak contains no tenderloin and is relatively small and compact with no bone.	Rare: Medium: Well done:	5 minutes 5—7 minutes 8—10 minutes		As for T-bone.
Entrecôte (1 inch thick, serves 1) Also called rib steak, entrecôte is a European cut from the first few ribs. It can be cut up to 3 inches thick.	Rare: Medium: Well done:	5 minutes 6—7 minutes 8—10 minutes		Maître d'hôtel or garlic butter; sauce Bordelaise; French fries or baked potatoes; braised endive; caramelized tomatoes; green salad.

Pan Frying

Some people prefer pan-fried to broiled steak and pan frying has an advantage because it can be done with a minimum of equipment on a single burner or in an electric frying pan.

Take a heavy skillet, plain or ridged, or a very heavy enameled iron or heavy aluminum frying pan. Set on full heat for several minutes or until very hot, then add 1 tablespoon of oil or meat drippings. When sizzling, add the meat. Keep on full heat until well browned on one side, pressing the meat well down with a metal spatula; turn and brown on the other side. (If using a ridged pan, the meat should be shifted during cooking and replaced at an angle so the surface is marked in a diamond pattern.) Then lower heat and cook until done. The frying time depends on what is cooked and how well it should be done.

Steak Cuts	Broiling Times		Accompaniments
Filet mignon ($1-1\frac{1}{2}$ inches thick, serves 1) Pan fry or broil this expensive steak. In Europe, the filet is detached and cut separately, not divided into Porterhouse and T-bone steaks, as we do here in America.	Rare: Medium to well done:	6 minutes 7–8 minutes	Béarnaise sauce or juices from the pan; French fries or straw potatoes; stuffed mushrooms.
Tournedos ($1\frac{1}{2}-2$ inches thick, serves 1) The center of the fillet, trimmed of all fat and surrounding meat; lard it with a thin strip of fat tied around the edge.	Rare: Medium:	7–8 minutes 8–10 minutes	As for filet mignon.
Chateaubriand (3–4 inches thick, serves 2) A cut from the thickest part of the fillet corresponding to the tenderloin portion included in Porterhouse steak. It can be broiled or pan fried; slice down for serving.	Rare to medium rare:	 16–20 minutes	Béarnaise sauce; château potatoes.
Minute ($\frac{1}{2}$ inch thick, serves 1) Correctly, minute steak is a thin slice of entrecôte, but the term has come to mean any very thin steak. Rapidly pan fry rather than broil it so it browns without overcooking.	Rare: Medium:	$1-1\frac{1}{2}$ minutes 2–3 minutes	Maître d'hôtel or garlic butter; French fries; green salad; watercress garnish.
Flank or London broil ($1\frac{1}{2}-2$ inches thick, serves 4) Flank is solid, lean meat and can be very tough. Broil only the highest grades and always serve it rare. It must be carved in very thin diagonal slices.	Rare:	10–14 minutes	Sauce Madère; baked potatoes; fried onions; broiled tomatoes; stuffed mushrooms.
Hamburger ($\frac{3}{4}-1\frac{1}{2}$ inches thick, serves 1) This can be ground from the round, chuck, sirloin, or the butcher's personal mixture — extra lean if you like.	Rare: Medium:	5–7 minutes 7–9 minutes	French fries or baked potatoes; uncooked or cooked onion; uncooked tomato.

Pan fried lamb chops are served with new boiled potatoes, sprinkled with chopped parsley

LAMB

Rib Chops

Ribs are the leanest lamb chops. Bones should be scraped clean of almost all fat, leaving a small solid piece of meat, surrounded by a little fat. A rib chop may have one or two bones, according to how thickly it is cut; if less than 1 inch thick, it will curl during cooking. Allow 2–3 medium chops per person.

Brush chops with oil, sprinkle with pepper and broil 7–8 minutes, turning once or twice, basting meat with oil. Chops should be well browned with fat, crisp on outside (many people like a touch of char) and delicately pink when cut. Sprinkle with salt; serve plain or with a savory butter such as tomato, orange or chutney. Good vegetables to accompany rib chops are peas, baby carrots or sautéed artichoke hearts.

Loin Chops

Loin chops are larger and more succulent than rib chops and have a T-shaped bone. They are sometimes 'butterflied' — that is, cut to double thickness, then split almost to the center and flattened to form a double chop. Allow 2 regular chops or 1 butterfly chop per person.

Brush chops with oil, sprinkle with pepper and broil 8–9 minutes (for chops which are 1–1½ inches thick) as for rib chops. They should be well browned but slightly pink when cut. Serve with any of the savory butters, especially chutney butter. Best vegetable accompaniments are green beans, ratatouille (from Provence, France, made with eggplant, peppers, zucchini and tomatoes — a recipe will be given in a future Volume), or buttered zucchini and small parsley or mashed potatoes.

Shoulder Chops

Lamb chops, frequently cut from the shoulder, are a good, economical choice, although they do not compare in flavor or tenderness with other chops. Cook and serve as for loin chops; if you like, brush during cooking with hot or blender barbecue basting sauce.

Noisettes

These are rib chops without the bone. To make them, buy boned rolled rack of lamb, well trimmed of excess fat; or remove bones yourself, using a small sharp knife, working in short strokes. Keep knife close to bone to avoid

Cut between tied sections to make a lamb noisette

cutting into meat.

When the bone is removed, season the cut surface of the meat and roll it, starting at the lean side. Trim the fat if there is more than enough to wrap once around the lean meat. Tie securely at 1–1½ inch intervals with fine string, then cut between each tie to make a 'noisette'. Allow 1–2 noisettes per person and broil 7–8 minutes as for rib chops. Noisettes look best when served on a platter with their accompanying vegetables (as for rib chops).

Kebabs

The traditional shashlik (skewer) dish consists of square chunks of meat, usually lamb, cut from shoulder or leg and threaded on long metal skewers, interspersed with slices of onion and bay leaves. A mixture can also be made with kidneys, mushrooms, bacon rolls and pieces of lamb or fillet steak. Impale these on a skewer, brush with melted butter or hot barbecue sauce and broil, turning skewer to cook chunks evenly. If no sauce is used, season the kebabs after cooking.

Kebabs are generally served on a bed of boiled rice or pilaf.

Kidneys

Kidneys make a delicious and unusual broiled dish. If kidneys have not been skinned, pierce skin on rounded side and draw it back towards the core. Pull it gently to get out as much of the core as possible; then cut away the skin and snip the tubes with scissors. Split open the rounded side and thread on a skewer to keep flat. Two or three kidneys are needed for each serving. Sprinkle with pepper, brush with melted butter, and broil, rounded side towards the heat at first, for 6–8 minutes, depending on size. Turn once during cooking.

Watchpoint: brush kidneys from time to time with melted butter to prevent them from becoming dry. Do not overcook or they will be leathery. Add salt and serve kidneys with maître d'hôtel, or anchovy, butter.

To prepare kidney, remove the skin and cut the ducts with scissors. Slit kidney in half lengthwise with a knife to cut out the core

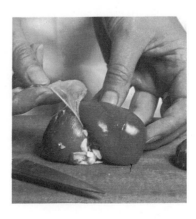

Mixed grill is a delicious way of serving a selection of broiled foods

Mixed Grill

A mixed grill consists of a combination of broiled foods and usually includes for each person a lamb rib chop, 1 lamb kidney, 1 country sausage, 1–2 slices bacon, 1 tomato, 2–3 large mushrooms, watercress for garnish and maître d'hôtel butter. Sometimes a small fillet steak is added as well.

First prepare kidneys and rib chops as described on page 75. Halve tomato and season the cut surface. Cut mushroom stems level with caps. Wash and pick over the watercress, discarding thick stems. Prepare maître d'hôtel butter and chill. Heat broiler or light the barbecue.

Broil tomatoes, rounded side to the heat for 3–4 minutes. Turn them, sprinkle with sugar, add a piece of butter and broil again for 3–4 minutes. Broil mushrooms in the same way (without sugar), putting a piece of butter on each side. Arrange on a platter and keep hot, or shift to the side of the barbecue rack.

Broil bacon, then sausages, turning them once. Add to mushrooms and tomatoes.

Broil chops and kidneys and add to the dish. Top the kidneys with maître d'hôtel butter, garnish with watercress and serve hot. Serve French fries, if you like.

Mushroom stems should not be discarded. Chop them finely, cook in butter until dry and store in an airtight container in the refrigerator (they will keep 8–10 days). Use in sauces, omelets, scrambled eggs and soups for a good flavor.

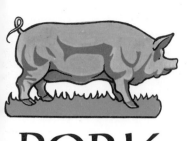

PORK

Pork Chops

Pork must be so thoroughly cooked that many people do not recommend broiling chops, maintaining that the long cooking necessary dries the meat. However, pork chops can be broiled successfully if they are basted often during cooking.

The chops should be neatly trimmed and any surplus fat removed before brushing with melted butter. Heat broiler and cook chops thoroughly, allowing 5–7 minutes on each side and seasoning after cooking. Brush with butter or sweet and sour barbecue sauce during cooking. Two chops per person is an average serving.

Serve with apple or tomato soy sauce if the chops are plainly broiled with butter, or with fried apple slices if they have been basted with sauce during cooking. Garnish with watercress and serve sautéed potatoes separately.

A salad is better than a cooked vegetable accompaniment. If serving with tomato soy sauce, spoon a little over the base of the platter, arrange the chops down the center and serve the remaining sauce separately.

Spareribs

The best part of spareribs are the long bones, which should have plenty of meat between them. Even so, allow 1 lb or more ribs per person. They must be cooked slowly for a long time so that the fat is drained. This is possible to achieve on a barbecue, but the ribs must be basted often as they dry out easily. A safer method is to parboil the ribs for 30 minutes, or until just tender, or to roast them in a moderate oven (350°F) for 45 minutes. Cut them in serving pieces and then broil 10–15 minutes, basting often with oil or sweet and sour sauce, until they are crisp and brown, turning once.

Serve spareribs with baked potatoes or French bread and a green salad.

Ham Steaks

Uncooked ham is best for broiling and it should be cut about $\frac{1}{2}$ inch thick. Allow about 7–8 minutes on each side and baste ham often with melted butter or a sweet and sour, or blender, barbecue sauce.

If using sweet and sour sauce, garnish ham with a slice of fresh pineapple and serve with boiled rice or hominy. Otherwise serve with leaf or creamed spinach and sautéed potatoes.

The term **barbecue** is said to have come from Florida, where French settlers spit-roasted goats 'de barbe en queue' (from head to tail).

Chops

Veal is a young meat with very little fat so it must be broiled with great care if it is not to be dry and tough. Loin chops are the only suitable cut for broiling.

The chops should be about 1 inch thick and cooked slowly until well done with no trace of pink – allow 7–8 minutes on each side. Brush meat often during cooking with melted butter or barbecue basting sauce.

If the chop is cut from the rib end, it may include a slice of kidney, surrounded by a thick layer of fat. (This kidney is usually removed and sold separately, so ask the butcher to prepare it especially.) The layer of fat around the kidney adds flavor and richness during cooking. One chop per person is enough. If not using a basting sauce, season chops and garnish them with maître d'hôtel or orange butter. Serve with sautéed potatoes and buttered zucchini, or green beans.

Kidneys

Veal kidneys are generally regarded as the best of all and they are superb when quickly broiled so that the juices are sealed in and the insides remain pink and tender. Allow 1 kidney per person.

Peel transparent skin from kidney and, with scissors, carefully snip away as much of the core as possible without destroying the kidney's shape. Flatten the kidney, brush with melted or herb butter and broil, rounded side towards the heat at first, allowing 5–7 minutes on each side.

Sprinkle with seasoning, transfer to a hot platter and top with maître d'hôtel butter. Best accompaniments are mashed potatoes, broiled tomatoes and mushrooms, and a green salad.

77

Broiled fish — the fish barbecue rack is the best way to keep fish whole when broiling or barbecueing

How to Broil
FISH

Small whole fish are excellent broiled and look as good as they taste.

Rich fish like mackerel or shad are best for broiling, but white fish are good, too, if they are generously basted during cooking with melted butter. Clarified butter gives a better color to the cooked fish. When broiling round fish, slash diagonally (score them) on each side 2—3 times so the heat can penetrate, shortening the cooking time. Flat fish need not be scored unless they are very large.

Fish steaks are also popular for broiling — the rich meaty texture of salmon and swordfish is ideal. It is possible to broil fish fillets, but they need frequent basting since they dry out very quickly.

Broiling times depend on the thickness of the fish, not on the weight. Fish should not be salted before broiling, but served with various savory butters, such as maître d'hôtel, anchovy or orange butter, which add seasoning; watercress is the classic garnish.

Broiled mackerel are scored and trimmed before broiling

Mackerel

Wash and dry fish, trim fins and 'vandyke' the tail, i.e. cut a 'V' shape, but do not remove the head. Score fish 3 times on each side and brush with oil or melted butter. Broil 5–8 minutes on each side, or until fish flakes easily when tested with a fork. Baste often. For mackerel fillets, allow 3 minutes on skin side and 8–10 minutes on cut side.

Serve with maître d'hôtel butter and/or quarters or slices of lemon.

Halibut Steaks

Halibut is an excellent fish for broiling as it is firm-fleshed and does not break up easily when being turned. Allow a $\frac{1}{2}$ lb steak per person. For an even brown color, dip fish in a little milk, then roll in seasoned flour before brushing with melted or clarified butter. For steaks $\frac{3}{4}$–1 inch thick, broil 4–5 minutes on each side, or until fish flakes easily, basting often with butter. Serve with maître d'hôtel, anchovy or orange butter, or Venetian sauce (see Volume 2).

Flounder and Whitefish

Small, whole flounder or whitefish of about 1 lb will serve 1 person. Fish should be skinned and the fins trimmed, but the head should be left on. Brush well with melted or clarified butter; broil 5–6 minutes on each side or until brown, basting often with butter during the cooking.

Pour over juices from broiler pan; top each fish with 1–2 pieces maître d'hôtel butter, or Venetian or Genevoise sauce (see Volume 2).

Trout

Wash and dry fish, trimming the fins. If fish are fat, score them, but if they are small, leave uncut. Brush with clarified or herb butter and broil 4–5 minutes on each side, or until the fish flakes easily when tested with a fork. Baste often during broiling.

If cooked with herb butter, garnish simply with watercress and lemon quarters; if cooked with clarified butter, add a savory butter garnish.

Shad and Sea Bass

Shad is full of bones and is best bought in fillets or split so all bones are removed before cooking. Skin should be left on as it holds fish together. Sea bass may be left whole for broiling and scored like mackerel, or they may be filleted. Allow $\frac{1}{2}$–$\frac{3}{4}$ lb per person, depending on whether or not fish is filleted.

For fillets, brush fish with melted or clarified butter; broil, skin side down at first, for 4–6 minutes on each side,

depending on thickness of fish, or until it flakes easily. Serve with maître d'hôtel or anchovy butter and quarters of lemon.

Salmon Steaks

Allow $\frac{1}{2}$ lb of fish per person and broil 5–6 minutes on each side; keep moist by basting with melted, clarified or herb butter. Serve with maître d'hôtel or orange butter; garnish with watercress. Salmon steaks are also delicious served with Hollandaise or Béarnaise sauces (see Volume 2).

BUTTERS AND SAUCES TO BASTE BROILED DISHES

Butters and sauces for basting should have a definite flavor as any subtlety is lost in the fierce heat of broiling. Cooked barbecue sauces for basting can often be kept for 1–2 weeks in the refrigerator, particularly if they contain vinegar; sauces which use fresh ingredients are best used within 2–3 days.

Clarified Butter

Clarified butter is the ideal fat for broiling. It has an incomparable flavor and does not burn easily because the water and salt content have been removed. However, it is extravagant because 1 cup of regular butter yields only about ¾ cup clarified butter.

To clarify butter: use at least 1 cup butter or more at a time as it keeps 2–3 weeks in the refrigerator after having been clarified. Cut into medium-sized pieces and melt in a thick saucepan over low heat. Continue to cook until foaming well, pour into a bowl and leave to settle.

After skimming any foam from the top, chill the clarified butter. It will have formed a solid cake on top and the liquid beneath (which is the water and salt) should be discarded. The butter may be used at once or melted down and stored, covered, in the refrigerator.

Herb Butter

To 1 cup clarified butter add 2 tablespoons lemon juice, 1 tablespoon chopped parsley, 1 tablespoon chopped chives and 1 teaspoon chopped thyme or tarragon (optional). Try adding crushed garlic if basting meats.

Blender Barbecue Sauce

For 2 cup quantity
1 cup tomato sauce
½ cup olive oil
2 cloves of garlic, chopped
¼ cup chopped scallions
¼ cup white vermouth, or lemon juice
1 teaspoon salt
½ teaspoon pepper
dash of Worcestershire sauce
dash of Tabasco

Serve with all meats and chicken.

Method
Combine ingredients; purée (half at a time) in a blender.

Hot Barbecue Sauce

For 2 cup quantity
2 onions, chopped
1 tablespoon oil
½ cup water
2 tablespoons vinegar
1 tablespoon Worcestershire sauce
¼ cup lemon juice
2 tablespoons brown sugar
1 cup chili sauce
½ teaspoon salt
1 teaspoon paprika
1 teaspoon black pepper
1 teaspoon prepared mustard
1 teaspoon ground chili pepper

Serve with steak, pork and game.

Method
In a saucepan, sauté onions in oil until brown. Add the remaining ingredients; simmer 20 minutes.

Sweet and Sour Barbecue Sauce

For 2 cup quantity
1 cup soy sauce
½ cup honey
½ cup sherry, or pineapple juice
3 cloves of garlic, crushed
1 tablespoon curry powder
1 teaspoon salt
½ teaspoon ground cinnamon
¼ teaspoon ground cloves
2 tablespoons chopped fresh ginger root, or 1 tablespoon chopped candied ginger

Serve with pork and chicken.

Method
Combine all the ingredients thoroughly.

BUTTERS AND SAUCES TO GARNISH BROILED DISHES

Cold savory butters can be shaped into squares by spreading the mixture ¼–½ inch thick on wax paper, chilling it, then cutting in squares. For circles, shape butter into a roll in wax paper, chill and slice. For butter balls, shape mixture with old-fashioned wooden 'paddles' made especially for this purpose (they are easy to use if first soaked in ice water).

The quantities given here are enough for 4 people.

Anchovy Butter

¼ cup unsalted butter
4 anchovy fillets (soaked in milk to remove excess salt)
black pepper, freshly ground
anchovy paste

Serve chilled with lamb chops and fish.

Method
Cream butter on a plate with a metal spatula. Crush or pound anchovies in a mortar and pestle, or a small bowl, and work in butter with pepper and enough anchovy paste to accent the flavor and give a delicate pink color. Shape and chill before serving.

Orange Butter

¼ cup butter
grated rind of ½ orange
1 teaspoon orange juice
1 teaspoon tomato paste
salt and pepper

Serve chilled with lamb chops, steaks and fish.

Method
Cream butter on a plate with a metal spatula and work in other ingredients with seasoning to taste. Shape and chill before serving.

Parsley Butter

¼ cup butter
1 tablespoon chopped parsley
dash of Worcestershire sauce, or squeeze of lemon juice

Serve hot with meat, fish and vegetables.

Method
Melt butter in a small pan and, when lightly browned, immediately add parsley and Worcestershire sauce, or lemon juice, and pour over meat, fish or vegetables.

Maître d'Hôtel Butter

¼ cup butter
2 teaspoons chopped parsley
few drops of lemon juice
salt and pepper

Serve chilled with steaks, mixed grills and fish.

Method
Cream butter on a plate with a metal spatula, then work in parsley, lemon juice and seasoning to taste. Shape and chill before serving.

Chutney, Garlic, Mustard or Tomato Butters

Make other savory butters as for anchovy butter, using $\frac{1}{4}$ cup unsalted butter with either $1\frac{1}{2}$ tablespoons finely chopped chutney, 2–3 crushed cloves of garlic, 2 teaspoons Dijon-style mustard, or 1 tablespoon tomato paste. Shape and chill before serving.

Barbecue Sauces

Many of the brown sauces described in Volume 2 are good with broiled meats – sauce chasseur and sauce Bordelaise are perhaps the most popular.

Rich sauces with a delicate flavor complement broiled fish and the butter sauces like Genevoise and Venetian in Volume 2 are ideal.

For a simple sauce to accompany broiled dishes try tomato soy sauce. Serve with most meats and with leftovers improved by a sharp sauce.

Tomato Soy Sauce

2 tomatoes, peeled, seeded
    and cut in strips
1 teaspoon flour
1 cup veal or beef stock
1 tablespoon soy sauce
dash of Worcestershire sauce
salt and pepper

This sauce is particularly good with lamb kebabs and pork chops.

Method
After broiling meat, pour fat from broiler pan, leaving about 2 teaspoons plus any sediment and meat juices. Stir in flour and cook very gently for 2–3 minutes until brown. Take from heat, stir in stock with sauces and seasoning. Return to heat and stir until boiling. Simmer 1 minute, add tomatoes and simmer 1 minute longer.

VEGETABLES TO SERVE WITH BROILED DISHES

To complement a steak, it is hard to beat a baked potato and a green salad, but here are other accompaniments suitable for serving with all types of meat and fish.

Stuffed Mushrooms

4 large, or 6 medium,
    mushrooms per person,
    and 2–3 extra
1 tablespoon butter
1 teaspoon chopped onion
1 tablespoon fresh white
    breadcrumbs, or 1 slice of
    bread soaked in milk
salt and pepper
1 teaspoon parsley
pinch of dried mixed herbs
little butter

Method
Choose mushrooms which are cup-shaped. Wipe with a damp cloth, if necessary, and remove stems. Chop stems with extra mushrooms. Melt butter in a frying pan, add onion with chopped mushrooms; cook over medium heat for 2 minutes, or until the moisture has evaporated. Take from heat; add crumbs or soaked bread, squeezed and broken up with a fork. Season and add herbs.

Pile stuffing into the mushroom caps, dot with butter and set in a buttered baking dish. Cover and bake in a hot oven (400°F) for 12–15 minutes or until the mushrooms are tender.

Roast Corn

4 ears of white or yellow corn
2 tablespoons sugar
$\frac{1}{2}$ cup melted butter
salt and pepper

Method
Pull back the husks from the ears of corn, but do not remove them. Pull off silk. Dissolve sugar in melted butter; brush corn on all sides. Sprinkle with salt and pepper; wrap in husks. Bake over barbecue coals or in a hot oven (400°F) for 25 minutes or until the corn is tender.

Fried Onions

1 medium onion per person
1–2 tablespoons oil or meat
    drippings
sugar (for sprinkling)

Method
Peel onion, slice a small piece from the side so that it stands firmly on the chopping board, and slice thinly across (not lengthwise). Push slices out into rings.

To make onion flavor less strong, blanch slices by putting in cold water, bringing to a boil and draining. Refresh under cold running water and drain on paper towels.

Heat oil or drippings in a skillet, add onions and sprinkle with sugar to help browning. Fry quickly, stirring occasionally with a fork. When very brown, drain on paper towels and serve piled around or on top of steak.

Preparing Onions

To peel an onion: first trim top and root, leaving enough root to hold layers together. Peel off first and second skins, or more, until onion is completely white. Try not to break the thin underskin – the oil released will make you cry. To skin baby onions easily, first scald in boiling water for 1–2 minutes, then plunge in cold water. The skins will peel off without trouble.

To slice an onion: halve it from top to root. Place a half, cut side down, on a board and, holding it firmly with one hand, slice evenly, with knife pointing from top to root.

To chop an onion: halve it and place cut side down on a board as for slicing. With knife parallel to board, make a series of even cuts from top to root, almost but not quite severing the slices. Make a similar series of cuts at right angles, with knife vertical to board. Finally slice across, to dice neat cubes, starting at top, and working to the root. The size of the cubes depends on how widely the series of cuts are spread.

*Good vegetables to serve with broiled dishes are
cucumber, yellow onions, scallions, zucchini, potatoes and mushrooms*

Buttered Zucchini

4–8 small zucchini
2–3 tablespoons butter
1 tablespoon water
salt and pepper
2 teaspoons chopped parsley
2 teaspoons chopped mixed
   herbs — basil, tarragon,
   thyme (optional)

Do not peel zucchini, but wipe with a damp cloth and trim stem and flower end. They are at their best when only 4–5 inches long and can be cooked whole. If larger, they should be cut into diagonal slices.

Method

If large, blanch zucchini in boiling salted water for 5 minutes, drain and refresh under cold running water.

Put them in a heavy-based pan with butter and water; season, press a piece of buttered foil or brown paper on top (this retains all the moisture) and put on lid. Cook over very low heat for 15–20 minutes or until the zucchini are very tender but still keep their shape. Sprinkle with chopped herbs and serve.

Lyonnaise Potatoes

The **Lyonnais district** of France is renowned for its potatoes and onions, along with other excellent foods and interesting regional dishes.

Method

Slice and fry one onion until brown. Remove from pan and sauté potatoes as in recipe for sautéed potatoes. When brown, stir in cooked onion.

Sautéed Potatoes

1¼ lb potatoes
2 tablespoons oil
2 tablespoons butter
salt and pepper
2 teaspoons chopped parsley

Method

Scrub potatoes and boil them, unpeeled, until very tender. Drain, peel and cut them in chunks. In a large skillet heat oil and, when hot, add butter. Add potatoes and sauté until crisp and golden brown, turning occasionally. The potatoes will quickly absorb all the fat and should toast in the hot pan until brown and crisp. Turn occasionally so they brown on several sides, although it is impossible to brown them evenly.

Take from heat, sprinkle with salt and pepper and add parsley. Serve in a very hot dish.

Baked Potatoes

1 large, even-sized Idaho or
   baking potato per person
salt
1–2 tablespoons butter per
   person
few sprigs of parsley (optional)

Method

Scrub potatoes thoroughly and roll in salt. Prick the skins and bake in a moderately hot oven (375°F) for 1¼ hours, or until the potatoes feel slightly soft when pressed. Take from oven and cut deep crosses in the tops, pinching them to open the cuts and let out the steam. Put a piece of butter and a sprig of parsley in center of each potato and serve at once.

Watchpoint: potatoes should never be baked in foil as the outer skin cannot become crisp and steam will be trapped inside the potato, making it soggy instead of light and floury.

COOKING WITH HERBS & SPICES

Herbs are indispensable in the kitchen, but they must be treated with respect. Correctly used in small quantities, they add character to a dish, but many are strong and pungent and easily overwhelm other flavors.

If you have a chance to grow your own herbs, do so for they are less blatant than dried herbs, which tend to have a harsher flavor. Dried herbs are also stronger than fresh so quantities should be doubled when using fresh herbs. Many herbs are easy to grow outdoors and a few, like chives, will thrive in a pot on the kitchen windowsill.

Unless specifically stated, all measurements in the Cooking Course are for dried herbs with the exception of parsley, chives and mint, which are readily available fresh.

The Chinese and the Ancient Romans were trading in spices long before Christianity began. In these early times, meals depended mostly on what was in season and available locally (imports were few) and the average diet was boring and limited. Spices were invaluable for adding taste and variety to all kinds of dishes. And it is no coincidence that hot countries serve hot foods because spices have long been known as excellent aids to preserving food. They were also used a great deal in medieval medicine, especially in the times of great epidemics and plagues.

Most spices came from the East and their transport made them expensive and, therefore, precious. The cost of a pound of mace was the same as the price of three sheep, and guards in charge of the spice cargoes at the London docks had their pockets sewn up to make sure they didn't steal any. Yet, despite the high prices, spices were used by cooks in wealthy households.

Today, spices should be used for their own distinctive flavors, and not to disguise bad food or an indifferently cooked dish.

For useful charts indicating which herbs and spices go best with what types of dishes, see pages 88–91.

Know Your Herbs

1a	Fresh bay leaves	**6**	Marjoram	**11**	Summer savory	**16**	Florence, or root, fennel
1b	Dried bay leaves	**7a**	Apple mint	**12**	Tarragon	**17**	Italian parsley
2	Chives	**7b**	Regular mint	**13a**	Regular thyme	**18**	Poppy
3	Dill seed	**8**	Regular parsley	**13b**	Lemon thyme		
4	Fennel	**9**	Rosemary	**14**	Balm		
5	Garlic	**10**	Sage	**15**	Sweet basil		

TYPES OF HERBS

Anise
A sweet-smelling herb with feathery leaves producing aniseed. According to the Royal Wardrobe Accounts of 1480, the personal linen of King Edward IV was perfumed with anise. Its principal use is in the making of liqueurs, but it can also flavor cookies, cakes and breads.

Balm
The aromatic foliage of this plant smells of lemon. It is seldom used in cooking, but a large handful of fresh or dried balm, infused in boiling water, makes a good tisane (herb tea).

Basil
Also known as sweet basil, it is grown in all temperate countries. Its warm, sweet aromatic taste is reminiscent of cloves. Basil has a natural affinity for tomatoes and it adds character to almost all salads, vegetables and seafood.

Bay
The ubiquitous bay leaf is an evergreen member of the laurel family. It is a foundation flavoring agent of French cooking, used constantly in bouillon, soups, stews, meat, fish, poultry, and in marinades. Caution: bay leaf and laurel are the same word (laurier) in French, but laurel is poisonous.

Chervil
A delicate, fern-like annual (of the parsley family) scarcely known in America, chervil is sweeter and more aromatic than parsley. It is usually included as one of the herbs in the traditional 'fines herbes' blend.

Chives
This delicate member of the onion family grows well in a pot on the windowsill. Chopped fresh chives improve any food calling for onion. Delicious in egg dishes, with vegetables, and salads. Chives are imperative in vichyssoise.

Dill
With its delicate flavor dill is the herb to use with fish, either in a sauce, or chopped and sprinkled on top. It is excellent with fresh cucumber as well as in the famous pickles. Both stalks and seeds are used in pickles and the seeds only for flavoring salads and vegetables, particularly cabbage and squash.

Fennel
A perennial plant with a very strong taste, fennel must be used sparingly. It is good in fish dishes.

Fines Herbes
A classic blend of herbs, frequently called fines herbes in French cuisine are tarragon, parsley, chives and chervil. This delicate combination is used in cooking eggs, sauces and soups.

Horseradish
This hearty, perennial plant of the mustard family was known in 16th century England as 'red cole'. Its most important use is as a table relish with roast beef, oysters and tongue.

Juniper
Juniper berries are most commonly associated with sauerkraut, game, marinades, and gin. They are the dried fruit of an evergreen tree or bush and have a slightly bittersweet taste.

Marjoram
This spicy aromatic herb is used principally for stuffing, especially for lamb. Though classed as a half-hardy annual, it will grow 2—3 years without dying, and will seed itself under normal conditions. It is good when dried and mixed with thyme and savory. Dried wild marjoram is called **oregano** — origanum being the botanical name of all marjorams.

Mint
Spearmint, heartmint, peppermint, horsemint, lambmint — all these country names indicate a species of mint. And their uses are myriad: sauce, jelly, vinegar, salad, candy and other desserts, julep and tea.

Parsley
The most common herb of all, parsley was known in earlier days as the herb of health. Today it is used mainly as a garnish, but makes a fine gelatin, a good soup, is delicious fried with fish and gives a wonderful flavor to egg mayonnaise when freshly chopped. Parsley is available in supermarkets all year long.

Poppy Seed
The texture of poppy seeds makes them interesting and their flavor is nutty but subtle. They come from a different variety of poppy than opium and are excellent in pastries, desserts and coffeecakes.

Rosemary
One of the most fragrant of herbs, rosemary is available either whole or ground and is excellent with lamb and pork. Freshly chopped rosemary is surprisingly good sprinkled on a slice of orange. Rosemary was used as a magic charm against witches and the 'evil eye'.

Sage
This perennial herb is most often associated with turkey, duck or goose stuffing. It also has an affinity for pork and veal, due undoubtedly to the mild flavor of these meats, and it is added to some cheeses.

Savory
A useful herb that has an aromatic flavor similar to marjoram; savory is good in meat and poultry stuffings, and accents flavor in almost any tomato dish. But its real companions are the entire bean family, including peas and lentils.

Sesame
Sesame seeds did not achieve status in this country until it was discovered that they were one of the big sources of polyunsaturated fats. Even so, the seeds, toasted or untoasted, add a definite flavor to cakes, cookies, candies and breadbaking.

Tarragon
Fragrant tarragon leaves, fresh or dried, complement chicken, fish and egg dishes. Tarragon also makes an aromatic vinegar used in salads and sauces and without it Béarnaise sauce would be characterless.

Thyme
The flavor of thyme is warm, aromatic and pleasant and the varieties read like a poem — lemon, mint, orange, the golden-lemon, the silver, woolly stemmed and caraway scented, to name a few. Thyme is used in a bouquet garni and chopped in many savory stuffings.

TYPES OF SPICES

Celery Seed
This spice comes from a variety of wild celery known in Europe as 'smallage'. Celery seed gives a pleasant flavoring to soups, pickles, cheese and pastries; it is excellent, too, in hearty salads such as beet, potato and cabbage.

Chili
Chili powder is made from the ground pods of several varieties of Mexican peppers combined with ground cumin, garlic and oregano. Its main use is in chili con carne.

Cinnamon
Warm, aromatic spice used in foods such as cookies, cakes and breads, in pickling and in drinks. It comes from the bark of the cinnamon tree.

Cloves
The flowers of the clove tree are picked in the bud and dried in the sun to form the characteristic nail shape. In fact, the word clove comes from the French 'clou' which means nail. Either whole or ground, cloves have many uses both in savory and sweet dishes. An onion stuck with a few cloves is a classic flavoring for stocks, soups, stews and some sauces.

Coriander
A member of the parsley family and one of the first seasonings grown in America by the colonists, the whole coriander seed is used in mixed pickling spice; the ground form in curry powder.

Cumin
Strongly aromatic, cumin seed is an essential ingredient of chili powder and curry powder, and is widely used throughout Latin America. The growing popularity of Mexican-type food has increased demand for cumin.

Curry
Generic term for a blend of many spices including ginger, chili, coriander, cinnamon, fenugreek, turmeric, mustard, pepper and cloves. The blend varies in strength and proportion, depending on amount of chili. In India and the Far East people grind and mix their own blends, according to the type of food being cooked.

Fenugreek
Whole or ground, the seed has a slightly bitter taste, not unlike burnt sugar. It is added to curry powder and chutneys; its principal use is for flavoring imitation maple syrup.

Ginger
Hot, sweet, clean-flavored spice that gives zest to meat, fish, or fowl. It comes in root form, either preserved in syrup or dried, as a crystallized sweet variety, or ground to a powder. The powder is used in cakes, cookies, puddings, and breads.

Mace
Akin to nutmeg, mace is in fact the outer coating of the nutmeg kernel and the two spices can be used interchangeably. Mace can be bought whole as 'blades of mace' or in the ground form. Excellent in any dish using cherries, it also adds interest to many white sauces.

Mustard
The seed is often added to pickles and salad dressings. When the seeds are ground to a powder, this is used to make mustard sauce.

Nutmeg
Sweet, warm and highly spicy in flavor, nutmeg blends with sweet foods such as cakes, cookies, custards and eggnogs. The slightly oval nutmeg is about the size of a large acorn and is at its best only when freshly grated at home on a nutmeg grater.

Paprika
Paprika, the ground powder of the pepper plant, is the Hungarian name for sweet pepper and is used in many traditional Hungarian recipes. It varies in strength — from very hot to sweet and mild — but always has a definite flavor.

Pepper (peppercorns)
Dried berries of the plant Piper Nigrum, native to the East Indies. Black peppercorns have the outer husk still on them; white peppercorns (milder than black) have the outer husk removed. Buy them in small quantities and grind them at home in a peppermill. They will keep their flavor for several years. If peppercorns need to be removed before serving, tie in a piece of cheesecloth.

Pepper (ground, black or white)
Either of these produces a less pungent and aromatic result than whole peppercorns. Buy ground pepper in small quantities since it loses flavor quickly. Use white pepper to season foods when specks of black pepper would spoil the appearance of the finished dish.

Saffron
The most expensive spice, saffron comes from the dried stigmas of the autumn crocus and each stigma is picked by hand. Happily, a little goes a long way. Saffron has an affinity for rice, and thus is important in such dishes as paella, and seafood pilaf.

Turmeric
Spice from the dried root of a tropical plant closely related to the ginger family. It is used in pickle and relish recipes. However, its outstanding use is to give color and flavor to curry powder.

Allspice
Berry of the allspice tree is one of the few spices native to the Western Hemisphere. Pungent and aromatic, allspice is used primarily in pickling liquids, marinades, spice and fruit cakes.

Capers
They are unopened flower buds growing wild on mountain slopes, mainly along the Mediterranean; they are sold packed in salt or vinegar. Use in hot and cold sauces, with vegetables such as tomatoes, eggplant and cabbage.

Caraway
Holland is the most important source of this favorite flavoring for rye bread. Caraway is widely used in cakes, cheeses, cookies, and vegetable dishes such as sauerkraut, or ones using beets and potatoes.

Cardamom
Only the dried, ripe seeds of the cardamom plant are used; these give an aromatic touch to pastries, cookies, curry powders, some meat dishes.

Cayenne
Very hot pungent pepper that must be used sparingly. It is ground from one of the many varieties of the Capsicum and is native to America, but cultivated in most of the warm parts of the world. Cayenne is good with meat, egg and cheese dishes.

Herb Chart

	ANISE	BASIL	BAY	CHERVIL	CHIVES	DILL	FENNEL	FINES HERBES	HORSE-RADISH	JUNIPER
SOUPS		TOMATO & MOST OTHERS	☆	☆	☆	☆	☆	☆		
FISH		SHRIMPS & OTHER SEAFOOD	☆	☆	☆	☆	☆			
MEAT		LAMB, PORK, VEAL	☆				PORK, SAUSAGES		BEEF, TONGUE	
POULTRY & GAME			☆							GAME, MARINAD
STEWS		BEEF	☆			☆	LAMB			
VEGETABLES		GREEN BEANS, TOMATO DISHES		ASPARAGUS, CAULI-FLOWER	☆	☆	BULB, AS VEGETABLE			SAUERKRA
SALADS & SALAD DRESSINGS		GREEN & TOMATO		☆	☆	☆	☆			
EGG DISHES		TOMATO & FINES HERBES OMELETS			OMELETS	☆		OMELETS		
CHEESE DISHES				CHEESE OMELET, COTTAGE CHEESE	CREAM & COTTAGE CHEESE					
SAUCES	☆	PASTA, RICE	☆			☆		☆	SEAFOOD SAUCES	
PASTRY & BAKED GOODS	BREADS, CAKES, COOKIES						BREAD			
OTHER USES	LIQUEURS						LIQUEURS		MUSTARDS, PICKLES	GIN

...JORAM	MINT	OREGANO	PARSLEY	POPPYSEED	ROSEMARY	SAGE	SAVORY	SESAME	TARRAGON	THYME	
☆			GARNISH		MINESTRONE	FISH CHOWDER	☆			☆	SOUPS
☆		BOILED SWORDFISH	GARNISH	CREAMED SALMON OR TUNA					☆	STUFFINGS	FISH
...GE,	LAMB		GARNISH		ROAST LAMB, PORK	PORK, VEAL	MEAT LOAF		VEAL	STUFFINGS	MEAT
...ING ...OSE	☆		GARNISH	CHICKEN LIVERS	POULTRY STUFFING	STUFFING FOR DUCK, GOOSE, TURKEY	☆		☆	STUFFINGS	POULTRY & GAME
☆			☆							☆	STEWS
...TOES	PEAS	EGGPLANT, TOMATO DISHES	☆		POTATOES		BEANS, PEAS, TOMATOES		☆	ONIONS, TOMATOES	VEGETABLES
☆	☆		☆				☆	☆	☆	☆	SALADS & SALAD DRESSINGS
...ETS			GARNISH						☆	☆	EGG DISHES
...M ...E,						☆			CREAM CHEESE		CHEESE DISHES
☆	☆	PASTA SAUCES					☆		BEARNAISE & TARTARE SAUCES		SAUCES
...PIES				BREADS, CAKES, COOKIES,				PASTRIES, BREADS			PASTRY & BAKED GOODS
	CANDY, DESSERTS, DRINKS, JELLY, LIQUEURS, VINEGARS	PIZZA		BUTTERED NOODLES, PASTRY FILLING	PUNCH		VEGETABLE JUICES	CANDY, OIL	VINEGAR	HONEY	OTHER USES

INDICATES THAT THE HERB GOES WELL WITH THE TYPES OF DISH LISTED IN THE COLUMNS AT EITHER END AS WELL AS WITH THE SPECIFIC SUGGESTIONS THROUGHOUT THE CHART

	ALLSPICE	CAPERS	CARAWAY	CARDAMOM	CAYENNE	CELERY SEED	CHILI	CINNAMON	CLOVE	CORIANDER
SOUPS			☆		☆	☆			☆	☆
FISH		☆			☆					
MEAT	SAUSAGE	SAUCE WITH PORK		HAMBURGERS MEAT LOAF	☆	ROASTS	☆		HAM, PORK, SAUERBRATEN	CHILI, FRANKFURTER SAUSAGE
POULTRY & GAME	MARINADE FOR GAME	SAUCE WITH CHICKEN								
STEWS						☆	CHILI CON CARNE		☆	☆
VEGETABLES	YELLOW VEGETABLES	CABBAGE, EGGPLANT, TOMATOES	BEETS, CABBAGE, POTATOES, SAUERKRAUT			☆	☆	EGGPLANT		☆
SALADS & SALAD DRESSINGS		☆				☆	☆	☆		
EGG DISHES					☆	☆				
CHEESE DISHES			☆		☆	☆				☆
SAUCES		☆		CURRY POWDER, CURRY SAUCES	☆	☆	CURRY POWDER, CURRY SAUCES	☆	☆	CURRY POWDER, CURRY SAUCES
PASTRY & BAKED GOODS	SPICE CAKE		BREAD, COOKIES, SEED CAKE	PASTRIES, COOKIES		☆		☆	☆	☆
OTHER USES	PICKLING FRUITS & VEGETABLES		PICKLES, RELISHES			PICKLES, SANDWICH SPREADS		DRINKS, PICKLING, RICE PUDDING	FRUITS, PICKLING, PUNCH	PICKLING

Spice Chart

	CURRY	FENUGREEK	GINGER	MACE	MUSTARD	NUTMEG	PAPRIKA	PEPPER	SAFFRON	TURMERIC	
☆	☆	☆						☆	BOUILLA-BAISSE		SOUPS
	☆		SAUCE FOR SHRIMPS	☆	☆		☆	☆	SEAFOOD PILAF		FISH
	☆		BARBECUED MEATS, POT ROASTS	VEAL			HUNGARIAN GOULASH, PORK	☆			MEAT
	☆				CHICKEN SALAD		☆	☆	CHICKEN		POULTRY & GAME
☆		BEEF					CHICKEN	☆			STEWS
	☆		BEETS			CABBAGE, CAULIFLOWER, CREAMED SPINACH	MUSHROOMS	☆			VEGETABLES
					MAYONNAISE, SALAD DRESSING			☆			SALADS & SALAD DRESSINGS
	☆			☆		CUSTARDS, EGGNOG	SPANISH OMELET	☆			EGG DISHES
ROLE					RAREBIT SAUCE	☆		☆			CHEESE DISHES
ER, / S			CHUTNEY SAUCE	☆	☆	FISH SAUCES	CREAM SAUCES	☆	TO COLOR CHEESE SAUCES	CURRY SAUCES	SAUCES
			BREADS, CAKES, PIES, COOKIES	CAKES, COOKIES		CAKES, COOKIES, DOUGHNUTS			BREADS, CAKES		PASTRY & BAKED GOODS
EY S	RELISHES	CHUTNEYS, SPICE BLENDS		PICKLES, PRESERVES	PICKLING	RICE PUDDING	SAVORY RICE		PAELLA, SAVORY RICE	ADDS YELLOW COLOR TO CURRY & PICKLES	OTHER USES

ICATES THAT THE SPICE GOES WELL WITH THE TYPES OF DISH LISTED IN THE COLUMN AT EITHER END AS WELL AS WITH THE SPECIFIC SUGGESTIONS THROUGHOUT THE CHART

Brochettes of kidney, sprinkled with chopped parsley, are served on a bed of rice (recipe is on page 96)

Hold a BARBECUE PARTY

Take your pick from the menu of chicken, lamb chops, or kidney brochettes, or make them all. Serve with various vegetable dishes and finish the feast with a fresh fruit and almond flan.

The dark, rich flavors of barbecued kidneys and lamb chops call for an authoritative red wine. Those from the township of St. Estèphe, in Bordeaux's famous Médoc district, are known for their generous bouquet and bold flavor. The closest American counterpart to these French reds is the Cabernet Sauvignon wine from California's Napa Valley.

Deviled Chickens & Simla Rice

Barbecued Lamb Chops
Spicy Potato Salad

Brochettes of Kidney
with Bacon Rolls

Mixed Vegetable Salad

Almond Fruit Flan

∿

Red wine — St. Estèphe (Médoc)
or Cabernet Sauvignon (California)

Day before

Make deviled mixture for chickens and barbecue sauce for chops; store in jars in refrigerator.

Prepare the dough for the fruit flan; wrap in wax paper and refrigerate.

Morning

Marinate liver and kidneys for brochettes; thread meat on skewers, cover with plastic wrap and refrigerate. Reserve leftover marinade for basting.

Make glaze; bake fruit flan shell blind; brush with glaze; cool and cover in plastic wrap. Set aside.

Cook rice for Simla rice, and plain boiled rice. Drain and rinse. Spread out on a shallow platter, and leave to dry.

Prepare all vegetables for salad and store in plastic bags in refrigerator.

Trim chicken halves and refrigerate.

Make spicy potato salad. Keep at room temperature.

Assemble equipment for final cooking from 5:00 p.m. for supper around 7:00 p.m.

You will find that **cooking times** given in the individual recipes for these dishes have sometimes been adapted in the timetable to help you when cooking and serving this menu as a party meal.

Order of Work

5:00

Prepare fruit for flan, arrange it in flan shell and brush with glaze. Chill.
Complete vegetable salad and refrigerate.
Stiffly whip cream to serve with fruit flan and refrigerate.

5:30

Light fire if using a barbecue.

6:00

Put plain boiled rice in a buttered heatproof dish, cover with buttered foil and heat in a moderately low oven (325°F).
Heat broiler if using stove for broiling.
Complete Simla rice and, when very hot, pile in a buttered ovenproof serving dish, cover with buttered foil and keep warm.

6:30

Start broiling chickens.

6:45

Start broiling lamb chops and bacon rolls.

6:50

Start broiling brochettes.

7:00

Serve broiled meats with accompaniments.

Split each bird down the breastbone, using a sharp knife. Hold birds firmly while cutting through the bone with poultry shears

Deviled Chickens

2 small chickens, split in half
¼ cup butter
watercress (for garnish)

For deviled mixture
2 teaspoons salt
2 teaspoons sugar
1 teaspoon pepper
1 teaspoon dry mustard
1 teaspoon ground ginger
½ teaspoon curry powder
2 tablespoons chutney
1 tablespoon ketchup
1 tablespoon Worcestershire sauce
1 tablespoon soy sauce
1 tablespoon plum jam
dash of Tabasco
about ½ cup stock, or water

Method

Cut away the backbones and rib bones from the chicken halves.

Melt butter in a small saucepan and brush the chicken with plenty of the butter. Combine all ingredients for deviled mixture (except the stock, or the

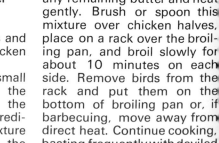

water) in the saucepan with any remaining butter and heat gently. Brush or spoon this mixture over chicken halves, place on a rack over the broiling pan, and broil slowly for about 10 minutes on each side. Remove birds from the rack and put them on the bottom of broiling pan or, if barbecuing, move away from direct heat. Continue cooking, basting frequently with deviled

Coat both sides of the chicken halves with the deviled mixture before broiling them

mixture, for about 5—7 minutes or until the birds are tender. Place them on a heated serving dish and keep warm.

Dilute the sauce left in the bottom of the broiling pan with a little stock or water and spoon it over the chickens before serving.

Garnish the dish with watercress, and serve Simla rice separately.

Quantities: if you make all the recipes in this menu you will have enough food for 8—12 people.

Simla Rice

1½ cups rice
¼ cup butter
1 medium onion, thinly sliced
1 teaspoon turmeric
salt and pepper

Method
Cook rice in plenty of boiling salted water for about 12 minutes or until tender. Pour into a colander to drain and rinse away excess starch with hot water. Let the rice drain thoroughly.

Melt the butter in a saucepan, add the onion and cook slowly until golden brown. Stir in the turmeric, leave to cook for 2 minutes and then add the rice. Toss with a fork while heating. Season with salt and pepper to taste and serve.

95

Barbecued Lamb Chops

8 loin lamb chops
1–2 tablespoons oil
(for brushing)

For barbecue sauce
2 large tart apples, pared and cored
1 medium onion
$\frac{1}{2}$ cup ketchup
2 tablespoons brown sugar
$\frac{1}{2}$ teaspoon salt
$\frac{1}{4}$ teaspoon pepper
$\frac{1}{4}$ cup butter

Method

Brush the chops with the oil and let them stand for about 2 hours at room temperature.

To prepare sauce: grate or finely chop apples and onion into a saucepan. Stir in all remaining ingredients and bring to a boil; simmer 2–3 minutes.

Broil lamb chops for 3 minutes on each side, spoon a little of the barbecue sauce over them and continue broiling 3 minutes longer, or until the sauce is brown and sticky. Serve chops hot with the remaining sauce in a sauce boat, and with a spicy potato salad.

Bacon Rolls

Allow 1 slice of bacon per person. Press slices with the side of a heavy knife to make them as thin as possible. Cut in half, then spread with Dijon-style mustard. Roll up each strip and thread on a skewer. Broil or bake bacon rolls until crisp and brown and then drain them on paper towels.

Brochettes of Kidney

allow 1 skewer with the following ingredients per person:
2 lambs' kidneys
2–3 squares lambs' or veal liver
chopped parsley (for garnish)
boiled rice (to serve)

For marinade
2–3 tablespoons olive oil
1–2 tablespoons red wine
few sprigs of thyme
salt
black pepper, freshly ground

Kebab skewers

Method

Skin and split kidneys (see page 75), cut the liver into squares about 1–1$\frac{1}{2}$ inches in size, removing all tubes and membrane. Combine ingredients for marinade with salt and pepper to taste, add kidney and liver and let marinate for 2–3 hours.

Thread kidneys and liver alternately on the skewers and broil 6–8 minutes, turning once and basting with the marinade throughout cooking. Arrange brochettes on a bed of freshly boiled rice and sprinkle with chopped parsley. Serve with a bowl of crisp bacon rolls.

Spicy Potato Salad

3 lb potatoes
4–5 slices of bacon
1 tablespoon vinegar
$\frac{1}{4}$ teaspoon dry mustard
$\frac{1}{3}$ cup green pepper relish
1 cup mayonnaise
1$\frac{1}{2}$ teaspoons celery seeds

Method

Boil potatoes in their skins until tender. Drain and peel them while still hot. Fry bacon slices until crisp and brown, remove from pan and drain on paper towels. Crumble bacon and set aside. Add vinegar to the bacon fat in the pan off the heat.

Thinly slice enough potatoes to make a layer in the serving dish, sprinkle with dry mustard and 1 tablespoon relish. Cover with a layer of crumbled bacon; moisten with bacon fat mixture. Add a layer of mayonnaise and a sprinkling of celery seeds. Repeat the layers until all ingredients are used, finishing with mayonnaise.

Mixed Vegetable Salad

small head (about 1$\frac{1}{2}$ lb) green cabbage
2 medium carrots
4 stalks of celery
3 tablespoons oil
salt
black pepper, freshly ground
2 crisp apples
1$\frac{1}{2}$–2 tablespoons white wine vinegar
$\frac{1}{3}$ cup sour, or sweet, cream

Method

Shred cabbage finely and soak in ice water. Peel and coarsely grate carrots; wash celery, trim and cut into julienne strips.

Drain the cabbage very thoroughly and put it in a bowl. Add oil and toss well until all strips are coated. Add seasoning to taste.

Pare, core and slice apples. Add to cabbage together with carrot, celery, vinegar and cream. Mix until the salad is well blended, taste and adjust seasoning.

Almond Fruit Flan

1$\frac{1}{2}$ cups flour
$\frac{1}{2}$ cup sugar
$\frac{1}{2}$ cup butter
3 egg yolks
2–3 drops of almond extract
$\frac{1}{2}$ cup whole blanched almonds, ground

For filling
mixture of fresh fruit in season (e.g. pears, grapes, pineapple, bananas, strawberries, plums, etc.)
apricot jam, or red currant jelly, glaze (depending on color of fruit used)
$\frac{1}{2}$ cup heavy cream (optional)

10 inch flan ring

Method

Sift flour onto a board or marble slab. Make a well in the center and into it put the sugar, butter, egg yolks and almond extract. Sprinkle almonds over the flour and work ingredients together until they form a smooth dough. Wrap in wax paper and chill 1 hour.

Roll out the dough and line flan ring. Bake blind in a moderately hot oven (375°F) for 20–25 minutes, or until golden brown. Let flan stand for a few minutes before removing the ring.

While pastry is still warm, brush inside with glaze and let stand until cold and firm. This prevents the fruit juices from soaking the pastry.

Prepare and arrange the various fruits in the flan shell and brush with hot glaze. Serve the flan with cream, whipped until it holds a stiff peak, if you like.

Brochettes of kidney and barbecued lamb chops; behind are (from left) bacon rolls, spicy potato salad, mixed vegetable salad and barbecue sauce; in front is an almond fruit flan

Shellfish are clockwise from bottom left: scallops, shrimps, mussels, oysters, lobster, Cherrystone clams, scampi, Dungeness crabs, blue crabs, and a lobster

SHELLFISH (1)

Today the seasons scarcely affect the supply of fresh shellfish, thanks to refrigeration and rapid transportation. Shrimps and scallops are as close as the freezer department of the nearest supermarket, as most supplies are frozen. Clams are dredged all year with the exception of a few icy days in the depths of winter but oysters are at their best in cold weather. Crabs can generally be found in winter, although they are more plentiful and less expensive in summer; soft-shell crabs are only available May through September.

Shellfish can be used in many ways but one rule is common to all types: do not overcook. Many shellfish are tender enough to eat raw and quickly become tough if you do more than cook them lightly. When you add cooked shrimps or crab meat to a hot dish, simply warm through without cooking further. Do not try to keep shellfish hot for any length of time, but take from the heat as soon as cooked and serve immediately.

SCALLOPS

Two kinds of scallops are native to North America — sea scallops (the French coquilles St. Jacques) and tiny bay scallops, esteemed by gourmets. Unfortunately, both have been overfished and are becoming scarce and expensive. Even so, they remain a good buy, since 1 lb of their rich meat will serve 3–4 people as an appetizer or light entrée.

Whole scallops are always sold prepared, but good fish markets carry scallop shells, which make attractive serving dishes — treat them like heat-proof baking dishes and scrub them for use again and again.

Sea scallops take only 6–7 minutes to cook and bay scallops are done in an even shorter time. Like all shellfish, they should be simmered, never boiled (boiling makes them tough and tasteless). To test for correct cooking time, cut one scallop in half and if no transparent center shows the scallop is sufficiently cooked.

Sea or bay scallops can be used in all the following recipes; cut sea scallops in 2–3 even-sized pieces before cooking.

Sea Soup

¾ lb sea or bay scallops,
   coarsely chopped
1 tablespoon lemon juice
½ cup water
2 tablespoons butter
1 quart milk
salt and pepper
½ teaspoon paprika
1 lime, thinly sliced (for garnish)

Method
Sprinkle the chopped scallops with lemon juice and let stand 20 minutes. Add the water and bring just to a boil. Add the butter, milk, salt, pepper and paprika and bring just back to a boil. Serve at once with a slice of lime in each bowl for garnish.

Scallops Provençale

1 lb sea or bay scallops
2 tablespoons seasoned flour,
   made with a pinch of salt
   and a pinch of pepper
3 tablespoons olive oil
2 cloves of garlic, crushed
2 tomatoes, peeled and
   seeded and cut in strips
1 teaspoon oregano
½ teaspoon thyme
salt and pepper

Method
Toss the scallops in the seasoned flour until well coated. In a skillet heat the oil and fry the scallops over medium heat until browned on all sides, allowing 3–4 minutes for sea scallops, and 1–2 minutes for bay scallops.

Add the garlic, tomatoes, herbs and seasoning and cook gently for 5 minutes or until the tomatoes are tender. Serve with boiled rice.

Scallops Parisienne

¾ lb bay or sea scallops
½ cup white wine
1 cup water
2–3 sprigs of parsley
½ bay leaf
6 peppercorns
4–6 fresh globe artichokes,
   or canned or cooked frozen
   artichoke bottoms

For sauce
3 tablespoons butter
1 onion, finely chopped
1½ cups (⅓ lb) quartered
   mushrooms
3 tablespoons flour
½ cup milk
½ cup light cream
salt and pepper
¼ cup browned crumbs
¼ cup melted butter
mashed potatoes (for piping)
— optional

*4 scallop shells, or individual
heatproof dishes*

The classic recipe for scallops Parisienne has a mushroom sauce. Correctly mushrooms should be the tiny white buttons called 'champignons de Paris' which can be left whole; larger ones must be quartered.

Artichokes are included in this dish because they have a delicate nutty flavor that blends well with scallops.

Method
If using sea scallops, cut in 2–3 even-sized pieces. In a saucepan combine scallops with wine, water, herbs and peppercorns. Simmer 3–4 minutes.

To prepare fresh artichoke bottoms: trim stems level with base. Cook, uncovered, in a large kettle of boiling salted water for 35–60 minutes (according to size), or until a leaf pulls out easily. Drain thoroughly; remove leaves and hairy choke. Cut bottoms into four pieces.

To prepare sauce: melt butter, add onion, cover and cook over medium heat for 1 minute. Add mushrooms and cook briskly until tender. Draw aside, stir in the flour, strain in liquid from the scallops (it should measure 1½ cups), blend and stir until boiling. Boil 5 minutes to reduce, then stir in the milk and cream, with seasoning to taste. Add scallops and the artichokes. Mix carefully and spoon into buttered shells or individual dishes. Scatter with crumbs and sprinkle with melted butter.

Pipe a border of mashed potato on shells, if you like, before browning in a hot oven (400°F) for 5–7 minutes. Fix shells in place on baking sheet with a little mashed potato or set on cookie cutters.

Mashed Potatoes for Piping

Boil 3 medium potatoes for 15–20 minutes or until tender, drain and dry well. Mash or put through a sieve.

Gradually beat in ¾ cup scalded milk, allowing 1 cup to every 4 medium potatoes, with about 2 tablespoons butter, and season to taste. The potatoes can be kept hot up to 30 minutes by pouring 2–3 tablespoons hot milk over the leveled surface in the pan and then covering with pan lid. Beat again before filling into a pastry bag, fitted with a large star tube, and pipe thickly on the shells. Brown in the oven or under the broiler.

Note: if egg yolks are added to potatoes with the butter — stiffening and further enriching the mixture — this is the famous duchesse potato purée.

Scallops mornay — serve as an appetizer or light entrée

Scallops with red wine and mushrooms have a border of mashed potatoes piped around the shell and browned

Scallops with Red Wine and Mushrooms

1 lb bay or sea scallops
¾ cup water
squeeze of lemon juice
3 tablespoons butter
1 medium onion, finely chopped
1 cup (¼ lb) mushrooms, quartered
1 clove of garlic, crushed
2 tablespoons flour
¾ cup fish, or vegetable, stock, or liquid from cooking scallops
2 teaspoons tomato paste
salt
black pepper, freshly ground
¾ cup red wine
2 tomatoes, peeled, seeded and cut in 8 pieces
¼ cup browned breadcrumbs
¼ cup melted butter
mashed potatoes (for piping) – optional, see page 100
1 tablespoon chopped parsley

4 scallop shells, or individual heatproof dishes

Method

If using sea scallops, cut them in 2–3 even-sized pieces.

In a shallow pan, combine scallops with water and lemon juice. Cover and poach 3–4 minutes. Drain scallops, reserving the liquid. Melt the 3 tablespoons butter in a saucepan, add onion, cover and cook gently for 2 minutes. Add mushrooms, increase heat and cook briskly until tender. Take from heat, stir in garlic and flour, add the stock or cooking liquid from the scallops, tomato paste and seasoning. Bring to a boil, stirring, and simmer 2–3 minutes.

Boil wine in a small pan until reduced by about one-third. Add to the sauce and simmer a further 5 minutes.

Add tomatoes to the sauce with the scallops and spoon into shells or baking dishes. Sprinkle with the breadcrumbs, tossed in melted butter.

If using mashed potatoes, pipe on the shells to make a thick border before setting them on a baking sheet. Fix the shells in place on the baking sheet with a little mashed potato or set on cookie cutters.

Bake scallops in a hot oven (400°F) for 5–7 minutes or until brown. Scatter with chopped parsley just before serving.

Baked Scallops

1 lb sea or bay scallops
3 tablespoons melted butter
salt and pepper
squeeze of lemon juice
½ cup heavy cream
¼ cup fresh white breadcrumbs
4 slices of bacon (to garnish) – optional

4 scallop shells, or individual heatproof dishes

Method

Put 1 teaspoon melted butter in the bottom of each shell or baking dish.

Drain the scallops, quarter them if using sea scallops and arrange in the shells or dishes.

Season and add a squeeze of lemon juice. Spoon over the cream, sprinkle with the breadcrumbs and add the rest of the melted butter.

Bake in a moderately hot oven (375°F) for 8–10 minutes or until golden brown The tops may be garnished with a slice of broiled bacon.

Scallops Mornay

1 lb sea or bay scallops
1 slice of onion
6 peppercorns
½ bay leaf
few sprigs of parsley
3–4 tablespoons water

For mornay sauce
3 tablespoons butter
3 tablespoons flour
2 cups milk
½ cup grated cheese – half Parmesan, half Gruyère
mashed potatoes (for piping) – optional, see page 100
salt and pepper

4 scallop shells, or individual heatproof dishes

Method

If using sea scallops, cut them in 2–3 even-sized pieces.

In a saucepan, combine scallops with onion, peppercorns, herbs and water. Cover and simmer 3–4 minutes. Drain scallops, reserving the liquid.

To prepare sauce: melt butter in a saucepan, remove from heat, blend in flour and then milk. Stir over gentle heat until boiling. Strain in the reserved liquid from the scallops and boil 2–3 minutes to reduce. Remove from heat, let cool, then beat in the cheese a little at a time, reserving 2 tablespoons. Taste for seasoning.

Arrange scallops in buttered shells or individual dishes. Spoon over the sauce, scatter with reserved cheese and place in a hot oven (425°F) or under the broiler to brown for 5–7 minutes.

If you like, pipe a thick border of mashed potato on the shells before setting them on a baking sheet to brown. Fix the shells in place on baking sheet with a little mashed potato or set on cookie cutters.

Scallops à la Crème

1¼–1½ lb sea or bay scallops
½ cup white wine
½ cup water

For sauce
2 tablespoons butter
2 shallots, finely chopped
1½ tablespoons flour
½ cup heavy cream
salt and pepper
2 tablespoons grated Parmesan cheese (for sprinkling)
2 tablespoons browned breadcrumbs (for sprinkling)

4 scallop shells or individual baking dishes

Method

Put the scallops in a pan with the wine and water, cover, bring to a boil and poach 1–2 minutes for bay scallops and 4–5 minutes for sea scallops, or cook until scallops are just tender and the center is no longer transparent. Drain and reserve the cooking liquid; slice the sea scallops, and arrange sea or bay scallops in the shells or dishes.

To make the sauce: in a saucepan melt the butter and sauté the shallots until soft but not browned. Stir in the flour, strain in the reserved cooking liquid and bring the sauce to a boil, stirring constantly. Simmer 2 minutes, add the cream, bring back just to a boil and taste for seasoning. Spoon sauce over the scallops and sprinkle the tops with a mixture of grated cheese and breadcrumbs.

Just before serving, brown scallops under the broiler or in a hot oven (425°F) for 5–7 minutes.

CLAMS

Clams are a North American specialty, found in a profusion of varieties all along our shores.

On the east coast, two kinds account for the bulk of the catch: the hard-shell clam that can be served on the half shell or used in the famous New England chowder, and the soft-shell clam that is milder in flavor and usually steamed or fried.

More than 30 varieties of clams grow on the west coast but only the razor clam (which is unsurpassed in flavor), the Pismo clam and the large mud clam are sold in markets.

Clams come by the quart and by the dozen; 1 quart of clams serves 1 person when steamed, or yields about 1 cup of shelled clams.

To prepare: wash clams thoroughly in cold water, rubbing with the fingers or, if necessary, scrubbing them with a stiff brush to remove any mud and weed. The shells of live hard-shell clams should be tightly shut, so discard any that do not close at once when sharply tapped and any that float or have broken shells.

Soft-shell clams have a thick black neck that protrudes through the shell, so they are never tightly shut. However, discard any that gape open or have broken shells.

Rinse clams under running water. (Some authorities maintain that further cleaning is unnecessary while others advise soaking them for an hour in a bowl of lightly salted water to remove the mud from inside them. Then lift clams into a colander — any mud from the soaking will remain

Preparing Clams for Steaming

Wash clams in cold water and scrub with a stiff brush to remove mud and weed

Soak clams in lightly salted water for 1 hour to remove mud from inside shells

Mud from the first soaking is left behind by lifting clams into a colander to drain

in the bowl.)

If fresh clams must be kept overnight, store them in a bowl without water in the refrigerator or a cool place. Do not cover them as they must be able to breathe.

If storing clams for a day or two, cover with cold salted water (sea water if available) after washing; add cornmeal to feed and keep them plump.

Most clams are completely edible, but the black outer webbing on the neck of the soft-shell clams must be peeled off with the fingers before eating — the meat underneath is edible.

As well as being cooked, hard-shell clams can be opened like oysters and eaten raw on the half shell with a squeeze of lemon and a drop of Tabasco. When adding shucked clams to other seafood mixtures, heat them for only 3–5 minutes as they easily overcook and become tough and rubbery.

Clam Quiche

1½ cup quantity of rich pie pastry (see Volume 1)
6 strips of bacon, diced
6 scallions, chopped
4 eggs, beaten to mix
½ cup clam juice
1 cup heavy cream
¼ teaspoon cayenne
1 cup shucked, drained and chopped clams
1 tablespoon chopped parsley
salt and pepper

8–9 inch flan ring, or quiche pan

Method

Make pastry dough, line the flan ring or quiche pan and chill. Set oven at hot (425°F).

Fry bacon until soft, add scallions and fry until both are brown. Drain them and add to the beaten eggs in a bowl. Stir in the clam juice, cream, cayenne, clams and parsley with salt and pepper to taste. Pour mixture into the pastry shell and bake in heated oven for 10 minutes. Turn down the heat to moderate (350°F) and continue baking 25 minutes, or until a knife

inserted near the center comes out clean. Serve hot or cold.

Steamed Clams

4 quarts soft-shell clams
1 teaspoon salt
melted butter

Method

Scrub clams and wash them thoroughly. Put in a steamer with salt and ½ inch water and cover tightly. Steam over high heat for 6–10 minutes or until clams open, stirring once. Remove black outer webbing from necks of clams, discarding any which have not opened. Serve individual dishes of melted butter with the steamed clams. Strain the broth through cheesecloth and serve in a cup to accompany the clams.

Steamed clams are ready to serve

Stuffed Clams

2 quarts clams, any kind
2 tablespoons butter
2 shallots or scallions
   chopped
2 cloves of garlic, finely
   chopped
$\frac{1}{2}$ cup fresh white breadcrumbs
2 tablespoons chopped parsley
$\frac{1}{4}$ cup dry white wine
salt and pepper
2 tablespoons browned
   breadcrumbs
2 tablespoons melted butter

Method
Wash and clean the clams and steam them until they open; remove meat, reserving shells. Discard black outer webbing on necks (if soft-shell clams are used) and chop meat finely.

In a small pan, melt the butter and sauté the shallots or scallions until soft. Take from the heat and stir in garlic, breadcrumbs, parsley and white wine. Add this stuffing to the chopped clams and season to taste. Fill into clam shells and sprinkle with browned breadcrumbs, combined with butter. Set the shells on a bed of rock salt or on escargot plates to keep them level and bake in a moderate oven (350°F) for 15 minutes or until golden brown.

New England Clam Chowder

1 quart shucked hard-shell
   clams, with the liquor
$\frac{1}{4}$ lb salt pork, diced
1 large onion, thinly sliced
3 medium potatoes, peeled
   and cubed
$1\frac{1}{2}$ cups boiling water
2 cups milk
$\frac{1}{2}$ teaspoon thyme
1 tablespoon butter
salt and pepper

True New England clam chowder is made with hard-shell clams, often called quahogs or littleneck clams in New England.

Method
In a saucepan, fry pork gently until very crisp. Remove diced pieces, add onion to pan and sauté until golden. Add potatoes and water and cook over low heat for 10 minutes. Chop clams coarsely, reserving the liquor. Add chopped clams to the vegetables and cook another 3 minutes.

Strain reserved clam liquor through cheesecloth and heat it. Scald milk, add clam liquor and stir into clam mixture. Cover, and simmer chowder for 30 minutes. Add thyme, butter and fried pork with salt and pepper to taste.

SHRIMPS AND SCAMPI

A large portion of the shrimps sold are, or have been, frozen; they make excellent salads and go well in recipes where a sauce or other ingredients add flavor, although connoisseurs insist on the superiority of fresh shrimps when eaten alone in a cocktail.

Quick thawing toughens shrimps and spoils the flavor, so they are best left to thaw out overnight in the refrigerator; keep covered to avoid dehydration.

Never boil shrimps. To cook 1 lb of peeled shrimps, simmer 3–5 minutes (depending on their size) in salted water flavored with a stalk of celery. Unpeeled shrimps take about 5 minutes to cook; test them as soon as they redden – the best way is to taste one. It should be slightly resistant, not fibrous or spongy.

To clean shrimps, make a lengthwise cut in the abdomen and pinch out the intestinal vein. In some species the sand vein down the back must be removed.

Shrimps sold as 'small' have a count of more than 31 per lb; medium shrimps have 21–30 per lb, large shrimps 10–20 per lb, and jumbo less than 10.

There is a great debate about the difference between shrimps, prawns, scampi and the French langoustines; different names are used in different areas for the same fish. Whatever their biological attributes, from the cooking point of view, prawns, scampi and langoustines should be treated as large shrimps; the same recipes can be used for all of them.

Seafood Salad

$\frac{1}{2}$ lb peeled, cooked or
   uncooked, shrimps
1–2 tablespoons water
   (optional)
squeeze of lemon juice
   (optional)
1 can (9 oz) mussels, drained
1 small head of Boston lettuce,
   or escarole
$\frac{1}{2}$ cup vinaigrette dressing
salt and pepper
1 can (8 oz) back-fin crab meat
1 can ($7\frac{1}{2}$ oz) tuna, drained
   and coarsely flaked

4 stemmed glasses

Any combination of seafood, or shrimps only, may be used.

Method
If shrimps are raw, place them in a baking dish, add water and lemon juice, cover and bake in a moderately low oven (325°F) for 15 minutes or until cooked. Cool shrimps in the liquid. Open the can and rinse mussels if preserved in brine.

Wash lettuce or escarole and tear in pieces.

Make the vinaigrette dressing and season highly. Drain the shrimps; combine with the remaining fish in a bowl. Mix with dressing to coat the mixture well. To serve, combine the seafood with the lettuce and pile in individual glasses.

Seafood salad is combined with lettuce and served in individual glasses

Shrimps Frederick

1½ lb peeled, uncooked shrimps
1 small bunch celery, cut into julienne strips
¼ cup cornstarch
¼ cup oil
1 cup rice, boiled (for serving)

For sauce
2 onions, sliced
3 tablespoons oil
1 teaspoon curry powder
2 teaspoons tomato paste
2 cups tomato juice
salt and pepper
2–3 tablespoons chili sauce

Make the sauce a few hours ahead of serving, so the flavor can mellow. This sauce is also good with fried or broiled fish.

Method
For sauce: fry onions in the oil until starting to brown. Add curry powder and cook, stirring, for 1–2 minutes. Stir in the tomato paste, then tomato juice, season to taste and simmer 5 minutes. Take from the heat and add chili sauce. Reheat before serving.

Toss celery and shrimps with the cornstarch until thoroughly coated and shake to remove the excess. Heat oil and fry shrimps and celery over medium heat until golden brown.

Transfer to a hot platter, pour over the sauce and serve at once with the rice.

Boiled Dressing

1 tablespoon sugar
2 teaspoons flour
1 teaspoon salt
2 teaspoons prepared mustard
1 tablespoon water
½ cup each vinegar and water, mixed
1 egg
1 tablespoon butter, softened
light cream, or milk

Boiled dressing forms the basis for many sauces — including the piquant and Alabama here — as well as being served as a salad dressing on its own.

Method
Combine sugar, flour and salt and stir in mustard with the tablespoon of water. Stir into vinegar and water, bring to a boil and cook 5 minutes. Beat egg with the butter until thoroughly mixed and gradually pour on the hot vinegar mixture, beating thoroughly. Cook over very low heat until thickened. Cool, then dilute with cream or milk to the consistency of heavy cream. This dressing keeps well, covered, in the refrigerator.

Alabama Sauce

1 red or green pepper, cored, seeded and chopped
1 cup boiled dressing
1 clove of garlic, crushed
2–3 stalks of celery, chopped
¼ cup heavy cream
2 teaspoons prepared horse-radish
¼ cup chili sauce, or ketchup
salt and pepper
sugar
dash of Tabasco

Makes about 2 cups.

Method
Blanch the pepper in boiling water for 1 minute; refresh and drain. Stir into boiled dressing with the remaining ingredients. Season generously with salt, pepper, sugar and a dash of Tabasco. The sauce should have the consistency of mayonnaise.

Piquant Sauce

1 cup boiled dressing
1 tablespoon chopped gherkin pickles
1 tablespoon chopped parsley
1 tablespoon chopped green olives
1 hard-cooked egg, finely chopped
1 tablespoon wine vinegar
salt and pepper

Makes 1½ cups.

Method
Combine all ingredients and season to taste with salt and pepper.

Shrimps or Scampi in Batter

1½ lb peeled, uncooked shrimps or scampi
deep fat (for frying)
fried parsley (optional)
salt and pepper
Alabama, or piquant, sauce (to serve)

For fritter batter
1½ cups flour
1 teaspoon sugar
1 tablespoon oil
1¼ cups lukewarm water
½ package dry yeast or ½ cake compressed yeast
salt and pepper

Method
For batter: sift flour into a bowl with sugar, make a well in the center and add the tablespoon of oil and half the water. Sprinkle over the yeast and leave 5 minutes or until dissolved. Stir flour mixture, adding remaining water gradually to make a smooth batter. Season and beat well for 2 minutes. Cover and leave in a warm place 20 minutes or until well risen and foamy.

Dry shrimps or scampi thoroughly. Heat fat until very hot (375°F). Dip shrimps or scampi into the batter and drop them, one by one, into the hot fat. Fry, a few at a time, until golden brown and crisp. Drain well on paper towels and keep hot in a low oven with door open until all are fried. Garnish shrimps or scampi with fried parsley, if you like, and serve very hot with Alabama or piquant sauce.

Scampi à la Crème

1½ lb peeled cooked, or
    uncooked, scampi or large
    shrimps
¼ cup butter
2 teaspoons paprika
6 tablespoons sherry
4 egg yolks
1½ cups heavy cream
4 tomatoes, peeled, seeded
    and cut in strips
salt and pepper
1 cup rice, boiled (for serving)

Method
In a skillet melt butter. If
scampi are raw, fry them
briskly for 2–3 minutes or
until cooked. If they are
cooked, simply warm them
thoroughly in the butter. Add
paprika and sherry and cook
until it boils. Flame, then boil
the liquid until it is reduced
by half.

Mix egg yolks with cream
and strain carefully into the
pan, stirring constantly. Cook
over low heat until the sauce
coats the back of a spoon.
Do not let it boil or it will
curdle. Add tomatoes, heat
gently for 1 minute, season
to taste and spoon into a
warm serving dish. Serve with
boiled rice.

CRABS

Crabs are the second most
popular shellfish after shrimps,
and frozen or pasteurized crab
meat is sold all year. Crabs
are at their best in summer
when available freshly cooked
or in the shell.

A favorite for eating straight
from the shell are the large,
meaty Dungeness crabs from
the Pacific coast. Blue crabs
are smaller but have an
equally good flavor — the
delectable soft-shell crab is
simply a blue crab that has
shed its old hard shell, leaving
a soft new one.

Only the legs of the giant
King crab are generally available, although the meat in
the small body — known as
'rice meat' — is also edible.
The legs usually come frozen
in the shell or in cans as crab
meat.

In recipes, any kind of crab
meat can be used. It is important to pick over the meat
carefully; it often contains
pieces of shell and transparent
membrane.

She Crab Soup

12 live she crabs
2 tablespoons butter
1 onion, chopped
salt
black pepper, freshly ground
2 teaspoons flour
1 quart milk
1 cup heavy cream
dash of Worcestershire sauce
¼ cup sherry

Traditionally this recipe is
made with she crabs whose
eggs give a delicious texture
to the soup. These crabs are
available only in a few markets
in spring, but regular crabs or

even canned crab meat (about
2 cups) can be used instead.

Method
Cook the crabs in boiling
salted water for 15 minutes,
or until bright red and the
meat is cooked. Drain, pick
the meat from the shells and
put with the crab eggs in the
top of a double boiler. Add the
butter, onion, salt and a little
black pepper; cook 5 minutes
and stir in the flour. Scald the
milk and pour onto the crab
meat.

Add the cream and Worces-
tershire sauce and cook over
hot (not boiling) water for 30
minutes, stirring occasionally. Add the sherry, cook 2
minutes, taste for seasoning
and serve.

Scalloped Crab

1½ lb crab meat
béchamel sauce, made with
    3 tablespoons butter,
    2 tablespoons flour, and
    2 cups milk (infused with
    6 peppercorns, bay leaf,
    blade of mace and a slice
    of onion)
4 stalks of celery, finely sliced
½ cup shredded almonds,
    browned
salt and pepper
¼ cup fresh white breadcrumbs
¼ cup grated Cheddar cheese
2 tablespoons melted butter

Method
Make béchamel sauce and
combine it with crab meat,
celery and almonds. Season
and spoon into a gratin dish
or shallow baking dish. Combine breadcrumbs and cheese
with the butter and sprinkle
mixture over crab meat. Bake
in a moderate oven (350°F)
for 20–25 minutes or until
brown.

Maryland Crab Cakes

1½ lb crab meat
6 tablespoons butter
1 onion, chopped
1 cup fresh white
    breadcrumbs
3 eggs, beaten to mix
¼ cup chopped parsley
1 teaspoon dry mustard
½ teaspoon paprika
salt and pepper
little heavy cream
seasoned flour (made with
    ¼ cup flour, ¼ teaspoon salt
    and a pinch of pepper)
¼ cup butter, or oil (for frying)

Method
In a skillet melt 6 tablespoons
butter and fry the onion until
soft. Add to the crab meat
with the breadcrumbs, eggs,
parsley, mustard, paprika and
salt and pepper to taste. Stir
mixture, adding enough cream
so it will hold together.

Form 6–8 small cakes, roll
in seasoned flour and fry in
oil or butter over moderate
heat for 5 minutes on each
side or until golden brown.
Drain on paper towels and
serve at once.

Deviled Crab

1½ lb crab meat
1 onion, finely chopped
4 tablespoons butter
¼ cup fresh white
   breadcrumbs
5 tablespoons grated
   Parmesan cheese
3 tablespoons light cream
1 teaspoon anchovy paste
pinch of dry mustard
pinch of cayenne, or 2–3 drops
   of Tabasco
dash of Worcestershire sauce
3 tablespoons browned
   breadcrumbs
2 tablespoons melted butter
   (for sprinkling)

For garnish
3 bananas
3 tablespoons butter
squeeze of lemon juice
deviled crackers

*4 crab shells, or individual
   gratin dishes*

Method

In a skillet fry onion in 2 tablespoons butter until soft. Add remaining 2 tablespoons butter and, when melted, add mixture to the crab meat with the breadcrumbs, 2 tablespoons cheese, cream, anchovy paste, seasoning and Worcestershire sauce. Add more seasoning, if necessary – the mixture should be spicy. Fill into the shells or dishes, smooth the tops and spread with a mixture of browned breadcrumbs and the 3 tablespoons cheese. Sprinkle with melted butter; bake in a hot oven (400°F) for 10–15 minutes or until brown.

To prepare the garnish: peel the bananas and cut in thick diagonal slices. Fry quickly in butter until browned and sprinkle with lemon juice and a little cayenne. Arrange on the crab shells or dishes and serve with deviled crackers.

Deviled Crackers

matzo, or unsalted crackers
melted butter
cayenne

Method

Brush crackers with melted butter, sprinkle with cayenne and heat in a hot oven (400°F) for 5 minutes or until very hot.

Crab Louis

1½ lb lump crab meat
2 cups shredded Boston or
   romaine lettuce

For dressing
1 cup mayonnaise
¼ cup heavy cream, whipped
¼ cup chili sauce
2 tablespoons chopped green
   pepper
2 tablespoons chopped
   scallions
1 tablespoon lemon juice
salt and pepper
milk (optional)

For garnish
4 hard-cooked eggs, peeled
   and quartered
2 large tomatoes, peeled and
   cut in 8 pieces

4 individual bowls

Method

Arrange lettuce in bowls and pile crab meat on top.

For dressing: combine all ingredients and season to taste. Dilute dressing with a little milk if necessary; spoon over crab meat. Arrange the pieces of egg and tomato around the edge of the bowls.

Dressed Dungeness Crab

1 large cooked Dungeness
   crab
salt and pepper
dry mustard
2 tablespoons dry
   breadcrumbs
1 tablespoon cream

For garnish if serving cold
¼ cup chopped parsley
2 hard-cooked eggs
1 head of romaine lettuce
6 radishes, cut into roses
1 cup mayonnaise
buttered wholewheat bread

For garnish if serving hot
maître d'hôtel butter
   (see page 81)
hot toast

Method

Remove large claws from crab and set aside. Twist off legs, at the same time removing the body or undershell. Set aside. Take out and discard the small sac lying in the top of the big shell, any green matter, and the spongy fingers lying around the big shell.

With a teaspoon, scrape the brown creamy part lying around the sides of the big shell into a small bowl. Hold the big shell firmly in a cloth and break down the sides, recognizably marked. Wash and dry the shell. Now cut the body of the crab in half, extract all the white meat with a lobster pick or skewer and place in a bowl. Take care not to break off any fine pieces of shell. Crack the claws, extract all the meat and shred it; again avoid breaking off any fine pieces of shell.

Beat the brown creamy part until smooth and season well with salt, pepper and dry mustard. Add 2 tablespoons dry white breadcrumbs and moisten this with a little cream

if the mixture is dry. Arrange the brown meat across the middle of the shell with the white meat on each side.

If serving cold, decorate the crab with chopped parsley and hard-cooked egg (finely chop the egg white and push the yolk through a sieve). Make a circle of legs and lay the shell in the middle. Surround with lettuce leaves and radish roses and serve with mayonnaise. Serve buttered wholewheat bread separately.

If serving hot, wrap crab in foil and heat in a moderate oven (350°F) for 20 minutes or until very hot. Serve with maître d'hôtel butter and slices of hot toast.

Broiled Crab Legs in Herb Butter

2 lb King crab legs in the shell
½ cup butter
1–2 cloves of garlic, crushed
   (optional)
2 tablespoons chopped parsley
1 teaspoon basil
1 teaspoon tarragon
salt and pepper

Method

Melt butter and add garlic (if used), herbs and salt and pepper to taste. Place crab legs in a flameproof dish, pour over the butter and broil 10–15 minutes, depending on the size of the legs, turning once. Alternatively bake the legs in a very hot oven (450°F) for about 15 minutes or until brown. Split them down each side with scissors, loosen the shells, baste with the butter and serve.

Serve cold dressed crab with mayonnaise and thinly sliced and buttered wholewheat bread

For dressed crab, remove claws

Take lungs from the body

Break sides of the big shell

Put crab meat and egg in shell

Iced cucumber soup, marbled with cream, is sprinkled with chopped mint or parsley (recipe is on page 114)

VELOUTE, ICED & BISQUE SOUPS

The name velouté exactly describes this soup's consistency – velvety (from the French 'velours' meaning velvet). Like velouté sauces, these soups are made by adding a well-flavored fish, veal or chicken stock to a blond (straw-colored) roux. The soup is cooked and seasoned according to the individual recipe, then finished with a liaison of egg yolks and cream and, sometimes, a little arrowroot or cornstarch.

Iced soups, also, can have a creamy consistency and they are prepared in a variety of ways.

Bisques are also rich creamy soups, generally made from shellfish such as shrimps or lobster. They are finished with a rich liaison and may be flavored with a butter made from the fish coral.

Hot and cold soups may be presented in a tureen; but iced soups (in contrast to cold soups) are usually served in individual bowls on ice.

Velouté Soups

Walnut Soup

½ cup walnut kernels,
  preferably freshly cracked
1 cup half and half
2 tablespoons butter
1 small onion, finely chopped
2 tablespoons flour
4 cups well-flavored chicken
  stock
salt and pepper
2 egg yolks
6 tablespoons light cream
fried croûtons (for garnish)

Serves 6 people.

Method
Remove as much skin as possible from the walnut kernels and grind them in a rotary cheese grater or work them a few at a time in a blender. Scald the half and half, pour it over the nuts and leave to infuse for 30 minutes in a warm place.

Melt butter in a large pan, add onion and cook until soft but not browned. Stir in the flour and, when straw-colored, pour on the stock. Blend and bring to a boil, season and simmer 7–10 minutes. Add the walnuts and half and half. Mix egg yolks and cream and add a little of the hot soup to this liaison before blending into remaining soup off the heat. Reheat without boiling and adjust seasoning. Serve with fried croûtons.

Crème St. Germain

1½ cups shelled fresh peas
  (preferably old and floury)
8 scallions, chopped
heart of 1 Boston lettuce,
  shredded
3 cups well-flavored veal or
  chicken stock
salt and pepper
1½ tablespoons butter
1½ tablespoons flour
1 cup shelled young peas
1–2 egg yolks
6 tablespoons heavy cream
2 teaspoons chopped mint
  (for garnish)

This green pea soup may also be served iced. If so, omit the egg yolks and increase the quantity of cream to ¾ cup. Whip it lightly until it holds a soft shape before adding it to the soup.

Method
In a large pan combine scallions, lettuce, stock and 1½ cups peas. Season and bring to a boil. Cover and simmer 20 minutes or until peas are tender. Work the soup through a food mill or purée in a blender. In a pan melt butter, stir in flour and cook until straw-colored. Blend in the pea purée, bring soup to a boil, cover and simmer 5–6 minutes.

Cook the young peas in boiling salted water until just tender, and drain. Mix the egg yolks and cream, stir in a little hot soup and add to remaining soup off the heat. Reheat without boiling; before serving, add the young peas and sprinkle with mint.

Iced Soups

Vichyssoise

white part of 6 leeks, finely
  sliced
2 tablespoons butter
1 stalk of celery, finely sliced
2 medium potatoes, peeled
  and sliced
5 cups chicken stock
salt and pepper
¾ cup heavy cream
1 tablespoon chopped chives
  (for garnish)

This classic soup must be made with well-flavored stock and heavy cream. If leeks aren't available, use mild or Bermuda onions.

Method
In a large pan melt butter, add leeks, celery and potatoes and sweat them (i.e. press foil or silicone paper on top, cover pan and cook over very low heat) for 10–15 minutes, stirring occasionally, or until very soft but not brown.

Stir in the stock, bring to a boil, season, and simmer 12–15 minutes. Work through a food mill or purée in a blender. Stir in the cream and taste for seasoning. Cover the soup and cool. Whisk a few seconds, cover and chill.

Soup should have consistency of cream and be smooth and delicate. Sprinkle a few chives over each bowl before serving.

Iced Cucumber Soup

4 cucumbers
2 shallots or 1 medium onion
  finely chopped
7 cups chicken stock
¼ cup butter
2 tablespoons flour
salt and pepper

For liaison
3 egg yolks
½ cup heavy cream

For garnish
¼ cup heavy cream
1 tablespoon chopped mint
  or chives

This soup may also be served hot.

Method
Peel cucumbers and cut into ½ inch slices. Combine in a pan with shallots or onion and stock and simmer 15–20 minutes or until soft. Purée the mixture in a blender or work through a nylon strainer. In a kettle melt the butter, stir in the flour and cook until straw-colored. Pour on the cucumber purée and stir until boiling; season and simmer 2–3 minutes.

Mix egg yolks and cream in a bowl, add a little hot soup to this liaison and stir back into remaining soup, off the heat. Reheat gently until the mixture thickens slightly, but do not boil. Chill, covered with plastic wrap to prevent a skin from forming.

Whip the cream until it holds a soft shape. Serve the soup in chilled bowls; gently stir a spoonful of whipped cream into each and sprinkle with mint or chives.

Three different soups, clockwise from the top: iced vichyssoise, crème St. Germain and lobster bisque (recipe is on page 118)

Iced Hollandaise soup has a colorful garnish of cooked vegetables

Cream of Mushroom Soup

2 cups (½ lb) mushrooms
4 cups well-flavored chicken
   stock
1 tablespoon arrowroot (mixed
   to a paste with 1 tablespoon
   stock)
¾ cup heavy cream
1 tablespoon chopped chives

Method

Wipe mushrooms with a damp cloth. Purée them in a blender or work them through a food mill. Heat the stock, add mushroom purée, bring to a boil and simmer 2–3 minutes. Stir in the arrowroot paste and bring just to a boil. The soup should have the consistency of cream.
Watchpoint: if the soup is not thick enough, add a little more arrowroot paste.

Lightly whip the cream until it holds a soft shape; stir into the soup before chilling. Garnish with chives.

Avocado Soup

2 avocados
2 cups well-flavored chicken
   stock
¾ cup heavy cream
1½ cups plain yogurt
½ teaspoon grated onion
¾ cup tomato juice
salt and pepper
dash of Tabasco

Method

Halve the avocados, removing the seeds, and peel. Mash pulp with a silver or stainless steel fork until smooth. Beat in chicken stock. Whip the cream until it holds a soft shape, add to the soup and season well, adding a dash of Tabasco. If the soup is too thick, add a little more stock. Cover and chill thoroughly.

Hollandaise Soup

5 cups well-flavored chicken
   stock
¼ cup butter
¼ cup flour
6 tablespoons light cream
2 egg yolks
salt and pepper

For garnish
3 tablespoons shelled green
   peas
2 tablespoons carrot 'peas'
   (scooped from the carrot
   with a small vegetable
   ball cutter)
2 tablespoons turnip 'peas'

This soup may also be served hot.

Method

Melt the butter in a large pan, stir in the flour and cook a few seconds. Pour on the stock, blend and stir until boiling. Simmer 10 minutes and skim if necessary.

Meanwhile prepare the garnish and cook in boiling salted water for 8 minutes or until vegetables are tender. Drain. Combine cream and egg yolks, stir in a little hot soup and stir this mixture into the remaining soup, off the heat. Add the garnish, season and reheat the soup until it thickens slightly; do not boil. Cover and chill.

Crème Normande

2 dessert apples
2 tablespoons butter
1 large mild or Bermuda onion,
   chopped
1 tablespoon curry powder
2 teaspoons flour
4 cups chicken stock
2 teaspoons cornstarch
   (mixed to a paste with
   2 tablespoons stock)
¾ cup heavy cream
2 egg yolks
salt and pepper
squeeze of lemon juice
watercress (for garnish)

Method

In a large pan melt butter, add onion; cook until soft but not brown. Add curry powder and one apple, pared, cored and sliced. Cook until almost soft, stir in flour and cook 1 minute longer. Pour in stock and add cornstarch paste. Bring soup to a boil, stirring; simmer 5 minutes. Add a little hot soup to cream and egg yolk liaison stirred together in a bowl; return to remaining soup in pan off heat. Heat, stirring, until slightly thick, but do not boil; work through a fine sieve or purée in a blender. Season, cover and chill.

Pare, core and dice the remaining apple, mix with a little lemon juice; add to the soup just before serving. Garnish each bowl with a few leaves of watercress.

Almond and Grape Soup

½ cup whole blanched almonds
1½ cups (⅓ lb) seedless green
   grapes
1½ cups milk
3 tablespoons butter
1 small onion, finely sliced
2½ tablespoons flour
4 cups well-flavored chicken
   stock
salt and pepper
2 stalks of celery, sliced
2 egg yolks
2–3 tablespoons heavy cream
1 tablespoon parsley
   (for garnish)

Method

Scald the milk, add almonds, cover pan and leave to infuse for 15 minutes. In a large pan melt butter, add onion and cook until soft. Stir in the flour, add chicken stock, season and stir until boiling. Add celery and simmer gently for 15 minutes.

Emulsify the almond and milk mixture in a blender or work it through a fine nylon sieve. Strain chicken stock and add liquid to the almond milk. Reheat the soup, adjust seasoning and add a little to the liaison of egg yolks and cream. Return this mixture to remaining soup off the heat; reheat until the soup thickens but do not boil. Cover the soup and chill. Serve sprinkled with parsley and add a few grapes to each bowl.

Bisques

Chilled Shrimp Bisque

½ lb peeled, cooked shrimps, chopped
1 onion, finely chopped
2 tablespoons butter
6 tomatoes, peeled, seeded and chopped, or 1 can (16 oz) tomatoes
3 slices of canned pimiento, drained and chopped
2 teaspoons tomato paste
5 cups chicken stock
1 tablespoon arrowroot (mixed to a paste with 1 tablespoon stock)
¾ cup heavy cream (for serving)
a few peeled, cooked shrimps (for garnish)

This soup can also be served hot.

Method
Cook onion in butter until soft but not brown. Add tomatoes, cover pan and cook gently for 10 minutes or until the vegetables are a pulp. Add pimiento, tomato paste and stock, and simmer 10—15 minutes more. Add the shrimps and purée the soup in a blender. Stir arrowroot paste into the soup and bring just to a boil, stirring. Cover and chill.
Note: if not using a blender, work the vegetables and liquid through a fine sieve and add the shrimps, finely chopped, after the soup has been thickened with arrowroot paste.

Whip the cream until it holds a soft shape and stir into the soup just before serving. Pile the remaining shrimps in the center of each bowl of soup.

Chicken Stock

When cooking a whole chicken, make stock from the giblets (neck, gizzard, heart and feet, if available); never add the liver because it gives a bitter flavor. (The liver is better for making pâté or sautéed for a snack.) Heat a thick saucepan with scarcely enough fat to cover the base; then add giblets and an onion, halved and washed but not peeled, and 'dry fry' over a high heat until lightly browned. Remove pan from heat and add 1 quart of cold water. Add ¼ teaspoon salt, a few peppercorns, and a bouquet garni (bay leaf, thyme, and parsley). Cover and simmer gently for 1—2 hours. When roasting, you can make stock in the same pan as the chicken by browning the giblets and onion with the chicken as it roasts and then adding 1 cup of water.

Fish Stock

Blanch 1 large onion by putting into a pan of cold water and bringing to a boil; peeled and sliced; drain and refresh.

Melt 1 tablespoon butter in a large saucepan, add the onion and 1 lb washed fish bones, cover and cook slowly for 5 minutes. Add 1 carrot, peeled and sliced, 1 stalk of celery, sliced, 6 cups water, bouquet garni, ½ teaspoon salt, 6 peppercorns, ½ cup dry white wine and a slice of lemon. Simmer gently, uncovered, for 20 minutes. Strain the stock and measure. Makes about 5 cups.

Lobster Bisque

1—1½ lb live lobster
6 tablespoons butter
2 tablespoons oil
1 small onion, finely chopped
¼ cup sherry

For velouté sauce
3 tablespoons butter
3 tablespoons flour
5 cups fish stock
salt and pepper
¾ cup heavy cream

This soup can be made with 2 cups lobster claw meat, but the flavor a live lobster gives is incomparable.

Method
With a cloth held in the left hand, grasp lobster firmly by the tail, head facing to the right. With a pointed knife, pierce the cross on the shell 1—2 inches behind the eyes — this will kill the lobster instantly. Continue cutting down, severing the head, then cut the rest of the body in half. Remove the hard sac from the head and discard. Remove and reserve any black coral from body. Remove and discard intestine.

Make lobster butter by working the coral with 3 tablespoons butter; set aside. Heat the remaining 3 tablespoons butter with the oil in a large skillet or sauté pan, add the lobster, cut sides down, cover and cook for 5 minutes. Add onion and sherry, cover, and simmer 10—15 minutes more or until the lobster is very red. Take it out, remove the meat from the body, crack the claws and remove this meat also.
Note: if you like, some of the tail meat may be reserved for garnish; cut it in slices and add to the soup just before serving.

Pound meat in a mortar and pestle, or purée in a blender with a little of the stock.

To prepare the sauce: melt butter, stir in flour, pour on the stock and any juices from the lobster pan. Bring to a boil, stirring, season and simmer 5—6 minutes. Take from heat and add the pounded lobster. Stir in the lobster butter (or 3 tablespoons plain butter) in small pieces, and add the cream. Reheat without boiling, taste for seasoning and serve at once, garnished with the slices of lobster.

Chilled shrimp bisque is garnished with a few whole cooked peeled shrimps

STOCKING THE KITCHEN CUPBOARD

What your kitchen cupboard holds is a very personal matter, depending on the amount of space you have, the preferences of your family, and your overall shopping pattern. It's true that for some cooks supplies are just a phone call away, but somehow an assortment of canned, bottled and packaged food, all neatly stacked on kitchen shelves, gives a feeling of security.

The main purpose of the kitchen cupboard is to have at hand the basic ingredients and seasonings used in day-to-day cooking. Naturally foods such as milk, butter, fresh vegetables, fruit and meats will need to be supplied as they are used. Try to work out a rotating system for the canned goods, transferring the old cans to the front of the shelf as you stock up with new cans in the rear. Keep opened packages of foods such as rice, pasta, crackers and cookies in airtight containers. Arrange spices, seasonings and herbs in the darkest, driest section of the cupboard. To help you make practical, interesting use of our guide in stocking your cupboard, we give recipes on the following pages for three spur-of-the-moment meals, all straight from the cupboard shelves. They are simple, but still good enough to impress guests with your creativity and your cuisine.

KITCHEN CUPBOARD SUGGESTIONS

HERBS; SPICES AND SEASONINGS ETC.

Bouillon cubes or powder: beef and chicken flavor.

Cheese: grated Parmesan.

Chutney.

Herbs and spices: basil; bay leaves; celery seed; chives; marjoram; oregano; rosemary; sage; thyme; tarragon; black and white peppercorns; cayenne pepper; paprika; chili powder; cinnamon; cloves; nutmeg; ginger; allspice; curry powder.

Mustard: prepared; dry; Dijon-style.

Olives: green; pimiento-stuffed; black (if opened and not all used, pour off liquid and cover with salad oil. They will keep for 3–4 weeks).

Pickles and relishes.

Salt.

Sauces: Tabasco; soy; Worcestershire; chili.

Tomato: purée; paste; ketchup.

CANNED FOODS

Fish: anchovies; tuna; salmon; sardines; shrimps; crab.

Fruit: cherries, pitted and dessert varieties (when thickened with a little arrowroot or cornstarch they make an excellent sauce for ice cream or to serve with meringue); pineapple (for salads and curries); plums; mandarin oranges; peaches; raspberries; figs; pears.

Meat: ham; tongue; corned beef; pâté de foie; chicken; turkey.

Soups: beef and chicken consommé (also good for making stocks and quick aspics); tomato; mushroom; black bean; gourmet game and lobster, etc.

Vegetables: artichoke hearts; baked beans; kidney and green beans; beets; carrots (tiny French or Belgian ones); mushrooms, whole and sliced; small white onions; asparagus; tomatoes (assorted-sized cans); potatoes; peas (tiny French); pimientos (small can).

The recipes given here are for three impromptu dinners, all using supplies from our kitchen cupboard recommendations. The next time you have an emergency that demands more expertise than simply boiling an egg or opening a can of sardines, try one of these menus.

BAKING INGREDIENTS; DRIED FOODS; SUGAR AND FLAVORINGS

Arrowroot; cornstarch (for thickening).

Baking powder; baking soda; cream of tartar.

Breadcrumbs: dried white; cracker crumbs.

Chocolate: sweet; semisweet; unsweetened.

Dried fruits: apricots; prunes; raisins; candied cherries.

Extracts: almond and vanilla.

Flour: all-purpose and cake.

Gelatin: and flavored gelatine.

Milk: dried; evaporated.

Nuts: whole almonds; pecans; salted peanuts.

Pasta: macaroni; noodles; spaghetti.

Rice.

Shortening: vegetable.

Sugar: granulated; confectioners'; brown; cubes.

Vegetables, dried or dehydrated: beans; barley; lentils; mushrooms; instant mashed potatoes; split peas; onion flakes.

MISCELLANEOUS

Cookies: ginger; vanilla wafers.

Crackers: plain, to eat with cheese; graham.

Drinks: coffee (vacuum packed and instant); tea; cocoa.

Preserves: jams; jellies; honey; maple syrup; marmalade.

Juices: tomato; lemon; pineapple; orange; grapefruit; clam.

Oil: olive for salad dressings (keep in a cool place); vegetable for cooking.

Vinegars: red and white wine; cider for general cooking.

Wine: red and dry white for cooking (keep in small bottles and refill when necessary).

Artichokes à la Crème
Curried Shrimps
with Boiled Rice
Peaches and Pears
in Spiced Wine

Artichokes à la Crème

1 medium can artichoke hearts
2 cups béchamel sauce
Parmesan cheese, grated

Buttered ramekins, or
individual baking dishes

Method
Set oven at hot (400°F).

Drain artichoke hearts and arrange in buttered dishes.

Make béchamel sauce, pour over artichokes and sprinkle with Parmesan cheese. Bake in heated oven for 10–12 minutes or until top is lightly browned.

Curried Shrimps with Boiled Rice

1 can (13¼ oz) shrimps
1 cup rice
chutney (for serving)
salted peanuts (for serving)

For curry sauce
1 tablespoon curry powder
1 large onion, sliced or chopped
2 tablespoons butter
1 tablespoon flour
1¼–1½ cups stock (made from chicken bouillon cubes, or powdered or canned consommé)
1 tablespoon red currant jelly or apricot jam
squeeze of lemon juice
1 can (8 oz) tomatoes
salt and pepper

Method
First prepare curry sauce: fry onion in butter until lightly brown. Add curry powder to pan and fry 1–2 minutes more. Remove from heat and stir in flour. Add stock, return to heat and bring to a boil, stirring constantly. Simmer sauce for 15–20 minutes. Add red currant jelly or the apricot jam, lemon juice and tomatoes. Simmer mixture for about 5 minutes. Taste and adjust seasoning, cover and set aside.

Pour rice into a large pan of boiling water, at least 3 quarts to 1 cup rice. Boil, stirring occasionally, with a fork for about 12 minutes or until the rice is tender. Take care not to overcook. Drain in a colander, pour hot water over the rice to remove excess starch and drain thoroughly. Transfer rice to a dish; let dry in a warm place.

Put shrimps in an ovenproof serving dish and spoon over the curry sauce. Cover and heat in a low oven (300°F) for 15–20 minutes. Serve with boiled rice, chutney and salted peanuts.

Peaches, or Pears, in Spiced Wine

1 large can (1 lb 15 oz) peach, or pear, halves, drained
½ cup red wine
¼ cup sugar
pinch of cinnamon
pinch of cloves

Method
Heat wine and sugar together in a saucepan until sugar is dissolved. Stir in cinnamon and cloves. Pour hot liquid over peach or pear halves and chill in the refrigerator before serving.

123

Special Tomato Soup

2 cans tomato soup
rind of 1 orange
4 tablespoons evaporated milk
few chives, chopped

Method

Pour the soup into a saucepan. Cut the orange rind into a thin spiral with a vegetable peeler, then cut in thin shreds and add to the soup. Heat through. Before serving add 1 tablespoon evaporated milk and sprinkling of chives to each soup cup or bowl.

Tuna Pilaf

1 can (6½ oz) tuna, flaked
¼ cup butter
1 large onion, thinly sliced
1 cup long grain rice
salt and pepper
2–2½ cups stock (made from chicken bouillon cubes, or powdered, or canned consommé)
1 tablespoon butter (for mushrooms)
1 can (4 oz) button mushrooms
squeeze of lemon juice
1 sliced, canned pimiento, cut into thin strips

Method

Set oven at moderately hot (375°F). Melt 2½ tablespoons of the butter in a saucepan, add sliced onion, cover and cook slowly until soft but not brown. Stir in rice and fry for a few minutes, or until it looks transparent. Season with salt and pepper and pour in 2 cups stock. Bring to a boil, cover tightly and bake in heated oven for 20–22 minutes, or until rice grains are tender and stock has been absorbed. If rice dries, before it is cooked add more stock. When cooked, stir in remaining butter with a fork.

Melt the 1 tablespoon butter in a pan, add drained mushrooms and a squeeze of lemon juice. Toss over a brisk heat for 2 minutes, then stir in the tuna and pimiento with a fork. Season and cook 2 minutes longer. When ready to serve, put rice mixture into a ring mold and press lightly with the back of a spoon to make rice hold together. Turn mold out on a serving dish and fill center with tuna mixture.

Spiced Figs

1 large can (1 lb 15 oz) figs
1 stick of cinnamon
3 tablespoons brown sugar
¼ teaspoon ground ginger
¼ cup sour cream (to serve) – optional

Method

Pour figs and fig syrup into a large skillet. Add cinnamon stick, broken in half, brown sugar and ginger. Cook, uncovered, over a very low heat for 10–15 minutes, or until syrup thickens slightly. Spoon syrup over figs during cooking. Remove cinnamon stick.

Serve at room temperature or chill and spoon a little sour cream on top, if you like.

Mousse of Liver Pâté

1 can (4 oz) pâté de foie
½ teaspoon Worcestershire sauce
2 tablespoons brandy
½ cup heavy cream
toast, or unsalted crackers (to serve)

Method

Empty pâté into a bowl and stir mixture with a fork to soften it. Stir in Worcestershire sauce and brandy. Whip cream until it holds a soft shape and fold it into the pâté gently. Spoon it into serving dish and serve with strips of toast or crackers.

Baked Tongue with Chutney

1 medium can beef tongue
6 tablespoons Madeira or sherry
1 teaspoon dry mustard
½ teaspoon thyme
¼ teaspoon freshly grated nutmeg
pinch of ground cloves
chutney (for serving)

Method

Set oven at moderate (350°F).

Cut tongue into slices about ½ inch thick. Then add enough Madeira or sherry to mustard, thyme, nutmeg and cloves to make a paste and spread a very thin coating on the tongue slices. Arrange in overlapping slices in a shallow baking dish. Spoon a little Madeira on top and bake 18–20 minutes, basting frequently with more wine. Serve hot with chutney.

Spaghetti with Mushrooms

1 package (8 oz) spaghetti
1 large onion, finely chopped
1 clove of garlic, finely chopped
5 tablespoons olive oil
1 can (8 oz) sliced mushrooms
salt and pepper
¼ cup chopped parsley

Method

Sauté onion and garlic in oil until they are soft but not brown. Stir in drained mushrooms and cook until they are heated through. Season with a little salt and pepper and add parsley.

To cook spaghetti: heat 2–3 quarts water with 2 teaspoons salt in a kettle until it comes to a rapid boil. Put spaghetti into the water gradually so as not to disturb the boiling point. Boil for about 10 minutes, stirring occasionally to prevent sticking, or until spaghetti is tender but still has 'bite'. Drain in a colander, toss with the mushroom mixture and serve.

Peaches Cardinal

1 large can (1 lb 15 oz) peaches
1 can (1 lb) raspberries
sugar (to taste)
2 tablespoons kirsch

Method

Drain peaches, arrange in a serving dish and chill. Work raspberries through a sieve to a purée and add a little sugar to taste, if necessary. Stir in the kirsch and pour purée over peaches. Refrigerate until serving time.

Large-scale Cooking

At one time or another, most cooks face the awesome task of cooking for a large number of people. Whatever the occasion — a children's party, wedding reception, church supper or buffet dinner — special menus must be planned, allowing time for shopping and advance preparation to avoid last minute confusion. At the same time, food must have the usual high standards and creative personal touches found at small dinner parties. The key to successful quantity cooking is thinking ahead.

Points to Remember

1 Review the menu you plan to serve. Don't include foods that are difficult to keep hot like Hollandaise sauce. Reject those dishes that overcook easily — like roast lamb or beef. (It is far better to use the braising method.) And don't leave major preparations to the last minute.
2 Some recipes cannot be doubled or tripled in most home kitchens. Don't try to double cake recipes but follow the regular quantities and make several. Cookie recipes can be doubled, but tripling yields an unmanageable amount of dough, producing inferior cookies. Pastry is best when made in the usual quantity; make and repeat recipe for best results.
3 Rather than mixing salad greens in one gigantic bowl (the greens wilt and discolor), have the assorted greens ready, and the dressing and chosen garnishes prepared in advance. Then toss the salad in small batches as it is needed.

4 Plan menus with the weather in mind — don't serve an aspic on a day when the temperature is 90°F. The result would be chaos. On the other hand, even a handsome lobster salad isn't very appealing on a chilly night when a steaming oyster soup or aromatic beef stew would have been a better choice.
5 If the meal is to be served buffet-style, remember that everything must be easy to eat with a fork, spoon or fingers. A knife is awkward to use when both hands are not free.
6 Try to make food that will look as handsome as possible, even when it is cut into; use large serving dishes and garnish the food sparingly but in an interesting way.
7 Consider your refrigerator space; if it is limited, plan some dishes that can be kept at room temperature.
8 Make sure you have plenty of counter and work space. If necessary, put up temporary tables. Enough working space makes all the difference in the world.
9 Before you begin to cook, review the number of large kettles, pots and saucepans that you will need and make arrangements for borrowing.

Quantities to serve 25 people

Coffee
$\frac{1}{2}$ lb ground coffee, 4 quarts water. Allow 1 pint cream and $\frac{1}{2}$ lb sugar. (For advice on making coffee, see Volume 2.)

Tea
$\frac{1}{4}$ lb tea, $\frac{1}{2}$ lb cube sugar, $1\frac{1}{2}$ cups milk, 2 sliced lemons. Pour 3 cups rapidly boiling water over tea; brew 5 minutes; strain into serving pot; dilute 1 part tea to 8 parts freshly boiling water.

Bread and Rolls
Four 1 lb loaves of bread; 4 dozen small rolls.

Butter
1 lb; soften by creaming before spreading bread or rolls.

Meat
With bone, allow $\frac{1}{2}$ lb per person. Without bone, allow $\frac{1}{4}$–$\frac{1}{3}$ lb per person.

Poultry
Allow $\frac{1}{2}$ lb per person.

Vegetables
5 lb cabbage for salad.
6 large heads lettuce for salad.
6 lb tomatoes, sliced.
8 lb potatoes to be boiled and buttered.
7 lb green beans.

Desserts
Four 9 inch pies.
Two 9 inch layer cakes.
1 gallon ice cream.
$1\frac{1}{2}$ lb salted nuts.
4 quarts fruit compote.

Drinks
1–$1\frac{1}{2}$ gallons fruit punch.
8 bottles wine (6 glasses – 4 fluid oz each).
$1\frac{1}{2}$ bottles spirits (20 average jiggers – $1\frac{1}{2}$ fluid oz each).

KINDS OF CITRUS FRUIT

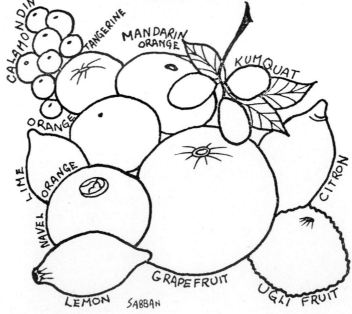

CALAMONDIN

TANGERINE

MANDARIN ORANGE

KUMQUAT

ORANGE

LIME

NAVEL ORANGE

CITRON

LEMON

SABBAN

GRAPEFRUIT

UGLI FRUIT

Lemons, tangerines, limes and oranges have nourished man for thousands of years with their vitamin-rich juices.

Originally native to Asia, citrus fruits were brought here by Columbus from the Mediterranean area, where the fruits grow in abundance. Grapefruit is the only citrus native to America, but all varieties of citrus fruits flourish here.

The citrus fruit trees with their dense evergreen leaves, exotic fragrance and white flowers, have long been extolled in print and painting as symbols of pure beauty.

We eat about 80 lb of citrus fruits per person each year — either as fresh, canned or frozen fruit or juice, or as peel and extracts.

The following are some of the best known fruits of the citrus family.

Calamondin
This small citrus fruit native to the Philippines is now cultivated here. Excellent for marmalade and used for artificial flavorings, calamondin is loose-skinned and extremely acidic with a high vitamin C content.

Citron
Known in Asia as early as 4th century B.C., this fruit is grown and valued for its fragrant peel. It has an oval shape with rough, yellow-green rind that is almost always made into candied peel. Candied citron peel, used extensively in fruit cakes and other desserts, can be bought halved or diced, in jars or by the lb.

Grapefruit
This is America's own citrus fruit, and is said to have started in the West Indies. The rind comes in shades from yellow to bronze to russet and pink. Good grapefruits are firm to the touch, heavy for their size and well shaped; their pulp comes with and without seeds, in pink and yellow.

Kumquat
The smallest of the citrus fruits, it looks like a miniature elongated orange. The rind is sweet and aromatic but the pulp is acidic and the entire fruit — rind and pulp — is usually eaten cooked. Originally the Chinese and Japanese used kumquat trees as decoration. Preserved kumquats come packed in jars and are available all year in many markets.

Lemon
A bright yellow oval fruit of the citrus family that is used in almost all categories of cooking — from soups to soufflés and in drinks and desserts. Many things taste better with a good squeeze of lemon accenting the flavor — particularly fish, veal and chicken. In many Mediterranean meat and vegetable dishes lemon often takes the place of vinegar and sometimes salt.

Lime
Bright green in color and shaped like a lemon, it has a distinctive tart flavor. Limes can be used interchangeably with lemons and add a particularly fruity zest to any dish. A common variety of the lime is the **Key lime** grown along the Florida Keys and renowned for its excellent taste in pies.

Oranges
Mandarin oranges are small round citrus fruits with thin, loose rinds. Both rind and sections of the fruit are easy to handle. Other types of mandarin oranges are **tangerines** and **satsumas**; satsumas are usually only available canned.

Navel oranges, one of over 200 varieties of orange grown in this country, are seedless and extra large in size. They are one of the best eating oranges because they are easy to peel and section and their flavor is rich and delicious. They are easy to recognize by the 'navel' or circular break in the rind at one end.

Bitter, Seville or sour oranges add a delicious tartness to orange preserves and they are used frequently for making marmalade. The sour, bitter pulp disqualifies them immediately for eating out of hand but when combined with sugar in cooking they add an inimitable mellow tartness to preserves.

The bitter orange tree rarely grows above 25 feet in height and is usually cultivated here for ornament rather than to be sold commercially. However, a small supply of the fruit is available in specialty markets in March and April. If bitter oranges are not available, substitute sweet oranges and decrease the sugar by one-third cup per orange.

Blood oranges have a red-orange rind with a pulp that is quite crimson. Grown mainly in Malta, Sicily and Spain, they are seen only occasionally in our markets.

Temple oranges, identified by their 'pebbly skin', are excellent eating oranges. Grown in Florida, they are available in markets most of the winter.

Murcott oranges, sometimes called honey oranges, are relatively new on the market. Basically an orange with many qualities of a tangerine and a pronounced honey flavor, they are excellent to eat.

Tangerines, a variety of the mandarin orange, are smaller than most oranges. They vary in color from deep orange to a red-orange and their loose rind makes them easy to peel. Select tangerines that are heavy for their size. The season, regrettably, is a short one — from November to March.

Tangelos
These are hybrids — a cross between a tangerine and a grapefruit (sometimes called a **pomelo**) — hence the name tangelo. They have an orange-like rind, usually deep yellow in color with pale yellow flesh. Tangelos are an excellent eating fruit.

Ugli fruit
Grown in Jamaica, ugli fruit is imported here in limited quantities. It has a rough, puffy unattractive rind with a delicious interior that tastes like an ideal combination of oranges, tangerines and grapefruit.

MEASURING & MEASUREMENTS

The recipe quantities in the Course are measured in standard level teaspoons, tablespoons and cups and their equivalents are shown below. Any liquid pints and quarts also refer to U.S. standard measures.

When measuring dry ingredients, fill the cup or spoon to overflowing without packing down and level the top with a knife. All the dry ingredients, including flour, should be measured before sifting, although sifting may be called for later in the instructions.

Butter and margarine usually come in measured sticks (1 stick equals $\frac{1}{2}$ cup) and other bulk fats can be measured by displacement. For $\frac{1}{3}$ cup fat, fill the measuring cup $\frac{2}{3}$ full of water. Add fat until the water reaches the 1 cup mark. Drain the cup of water and the fat remaining equals $\frac{1}{3}$ cup.

For liquids, fill the measure to the brim, or to the calibration line.

Often quantities of seasonings cannot be stated exactly, for ingredients vary in the amount they require. The instructions 'add to taste' are literal, for it is impossible to achieve just the right balance of flavors in many dishes without tasting them.

Liquid measure	Volume equivalent
3 teaspoons	1 tablespoon
2 tablespoons	1 fluid oz
4 tablespoons	$\frac{1}{4}$ cup
16 tablespoons	1 cup or 8 fluid oz
2 cups	1 pint
2 pints	1 quart
4 quarts	1 gallon

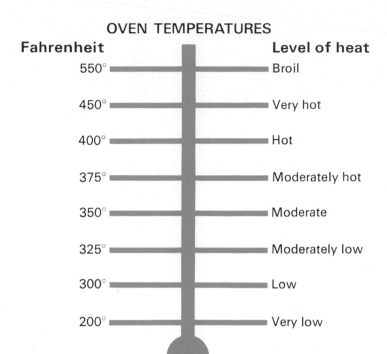

OVEN TEMPERATURES

Fahrenheit		Level of heat
550°		Broil
450°		Very hot
400°		Hot
375°		Moderately hot
350°		Moderate
325°		Moderately low
300°		Low
200°		Very low

OVEN TEMPERATURES AND SHELF POSITIONS

Throughout the Cooking Course, oven temperatures are stated in degrees Fahrenheit and in generally agreed levels of heat such as 'high' and 'moderate'. The equivalents are shown on the table above.

However, exact temperature varies in different parts of an oven and the thermostat reading refers to the heat in the middle. As the oven temperature at top and bottom can vary as much as 25°F from this setting, the positioning of shelves is very important. In general, heat rises, so the hottest part of the oven is at the top, but consult the manufacturer's handbook about your individual model.

Pans and dishes of food should be placed parallel with burners or elements to avoid scorched edges.

When baking cakes, there must be room for the heat to circulate in the oven around baking sheets and cake pans; otherwise the underside of the cakes will burn. If baking more than one cake in an oven that has back burners or elements, arrange the cakes side by side. If the oven has side burners, arrange cakes back and front.

Oven thermostats are often inaccurate and are unreliable at extremely high or low temperatures. If you do a great deal of baking or question the accuracy of your oven, use a separate oven thermometer as a check on the thermostat.

Cooking Curiosities

''It's as American as Mom's apple pie'' is a phrase that is now familiar around the world. Although the humble pie is not indigenous to the U.S.A., most people acknowledge the fact that American cooks can elevate what is basically a simple dish to new heights of culinary improvization and delicacy.

The first mention of fish or meat pies was originally made as long ago as the 15th century and it is a known fact that the wives of the Pilgrim Fathers brought more than just a new vision with them to Plymouth Rock. They also brought along the skill of the European cook and combined it with the native raw materials to produce such mouth-watering and satisfying concoctions as pumpkin and cranberry pies.

Key lime pie is another example of the improvizational flair of the American cook. This particular pie was originally created in Key West, Florida, using condensed milk. Condensed milk had first been manufactured in 1858 and it helped to alleviate the problems suffered by the South after the Civil War.

Although an elementary dish in principle, and one which is free of the stifling procedures that beset so much gourmet cooking, the pie lets the skilled cook make an individual contribution to the basic formula to provide a dish that is fun to cook, good to look at and enjoyed by everyone.

INDEX

(Volumes 1, 2, 3)

* = excellent recipe

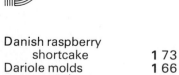

H

I J

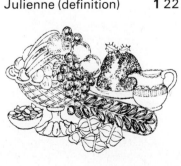

KL

MN

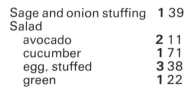

YZ

Notes

Acknowledgments
Photographs by Fred J. Maroon: pages 41, 48, 53, 94–95, 98, 104, 105, 116, 120. Other photographs by Michael Leale, John Cowderoy, Roger Phillips, Gordon McLeish and Gina Harris. Photograph on pages 44–45 by Syndication International; on page 107 by C. Délu/PAF. Shellfish information courtesy of National Fisheries Council, New York City.

Notes

Notes